DIGITAL
3D DESIGN

DIGITAL
3D DESIGN

Simon Danaher

THOMSON
™
COURSE TECHNOLOGY
Professional ■ Trade ■ Reference

First published in the United States in 2004
by Course PTR, a division of Thomson Course Technology.

For Course PTR:
Publisher: Stacy L. Hiquet
Senior Marketing Manager: Sarah O'Donnell
Marketing Manager: Heather Hurley
Associate Marketing Managers: Kristin Eisenzopf, Sarah Dubois
Associate Acquisitions Editor: Megan Belanger
Manager of Editorial Services: Heather Talbot
Market Coordinator: Amanda Weaver

ISBN: 1-59200-391-5

5 4 3 2 1

Library of Congress Catalog Card number: 2004106446

COURSE PTR,
A Division of Thomson Course Technology
(www.courseptr.com)
25 Thomson Place
Boston, MA 02210

This book was conceived, designed, and produced by
THE ILEX PRESS LIMITED
Cambridge
England

Publisher: Alastair Campbell
Executive Publisher: Sophie Collins
Creative Director: Peter Bridgewater
Editorial Director: Steve Luck
Design Manager: Tony Seddon
Editor: Stuart Andrews
Designer: Jonathan Raimes
Artwork Administrator: Joanna Clinch
Development Art Director: Graham Davis
Technical Art Editor: Nicholas Rowland

Printed in China

For more information on this title please visit:
www.cg3dus.web-linked.com

01

HISTORY OF 3D   6

02

3D IN THE REAL WORLD   24

CONTENTS

03 04 05 06 06

HISTORY OF 3D

Above: **In 1984, Apple's Macintosh computer introduced the first graphical user interface and the whole "desktop" metaphor, still in use in OS X and Windows XP today.**

PART 01. HISTORY

CHAPTER ONE

3D PAST

IN THE BEGINNING Computers have revolutionized the way we create and work with images and graphics. It's sometimes hard to grasp the vast, fundamental shift that technology has caused in the creation and distribution of visual media, especially since the actual workings of the technology still remain a mystery to many.

From the 7th through the 13th centuries, books—usually religious in nature—were created one by one by hand, and it took a huge amount of dedication to create such beautiful manuscripts. While the Chinese developed a form of simple printing at the beginning of the 11th century, it wasn't until the 15th century, when the German inventor Johannes Gutenberg (c. 1390-1468) invented his printing press using movable type, that the production and distribution of printed text and images in volume was possible.

Centuries later, printing was still done mechanically. Great newspaper presses could churn out thousands of copies bearing text and photographic images, and by the mid-19th century they were able to do so in color. Before any book or newspaper could be printed, however, the production and layout still needed to be done by hand first.

Then came the computer. A novelty at first, computers were created as counting machines and calculators for scientists and mathematicians. Soon simple displays were invented for displaying text and later graphics. Sophisticated interfaces were developed, and in 1984 Apple Computer released the Macintosh sporting its "desktop" metaphor interface. With the introduction of Aldus Pagemaker and laser printers, the desktop-printing revolution arrived and the rest is history.

The advent of personal computers featuring easy-to-use graphical interfaces was the spark that ignited the desktop-publishing revolution. This marked a huge change, enabling anyone with access to a computer to create and manipulate text and images. However, there were more than a few who were interested in images alone.

With the introduction of the Apple Macintosh and programs like Aldus Pagemaker (later to become Adobe Pagemaker) the role of the computer in publishing was set. With a computer that featured an easy-to-use graphical interface, it was simple to lay out text and images in the digital realm, then transfer them to an image-setter to produce color separations for printing.

The Postscript language bridged the gap between the computer and the real world, converting digital fonts and graphics into real printed text and graphics. Similarly, digital scanners took photographic prints or negatives and converted them into digital images for manipulation on the computer.

It was a program that could take digital images and make adjustments to them that sparked the digital-imaging revolution. Photoshop was designed by brothers John and Thomas Knoll to assist John in his work at the legendary special-effects company, Industrial Light and Magic (John would later become an important figure in the 3D industry, too). The program allowed simple color correction and file format conversion, plus basic painting and cloning tools. Suddenly it was possible to do pretty impressive things with digital images—things that were previously impossible. The digital darkroom was born.

Photoshop was licensed to Adobe and it has since become the most popular and important imaging program. It is also an incredibly important application for 3D artists, for whom it is used to create textures or composite 3D renders with other images.

The combination of Photoshop and early CAD (Computer Aided Design) software paved the way for new types of digital art. We can now use computers to generate photorealistic images using 3D software. We can combine 3D graphics with 2D photos or movie footage to combine computer-generated imagery with imagery from the real world. We can even take 3D objects designed in the digital realm and reproduce them in the real world through processes such as stereolithography and computer-controlled manufacturing. Increasingly, anything is possible.

Above: **Brothers John and Thomas Knoll developed Photoshop to help John with work he did at Industrial Light and Magic. After some initial difficulty in promoting the product they licensed it to Adobe.**

Left: **Arguably the most important software development in the graphics industry, Photoshop was the first program that could be used to manipulate images in a creative way. It spawned a generation of digital artists.**

EARLY 3D

While 2D graphics and desktop publishing were becoming established on the computer, 3D graphics technology was still only available to those in research labs at universities and large companies with powerful computers. Yet the development of 3D graphics could be traced back much further, to the 1960s.

In the early 1960s Charles Csuri, a traditional artist (and talented football player) became interested in the use of computers for creating images. Arguably the first "digital artist" he pioneered the creative use of computers in art, producing images and even animations as early as 1965. Working with mathematicians, Csuri even developed a way to plot 3D surfaces and recreate them in wood as sculpture.

Ivan Sutherland, working on his doctoral thesis at MIT, produced a program called Sketchpad for the TX-2 computer, then one of the most advanced in the world. He would later devise computer-graphics simulation systems for helicopter pilots, possibly the first "virtual reality" system ever.

In the 1970s computers became vastly more powerful and smaller. People like Jim Blinn, Martin Newell, Frank Crowe, and Ed Catmull at the University of Utah, and Michael Chou at NYIT, harnessed the power of the computer to devise ways to build models or real-world objects in 3D space inside the computer. Technologies that are still used today in computer-graphics programs were developed to "shade" the surfaces that were built and give them a photographic quality. Many of the advancements they developed are still in use today including shading, depth sorting, texture, environment and bump mapping, and antialiasing techniques.

Left: **Ivan Sutherland pioneered a lot of research into digital graphics and did so as early as the 1960s. He now works at Sun Microsystems.**

Above: **Charles Csuri was probably the first digital artist. In the early 1960s he developed the first computer-generated artworks.**

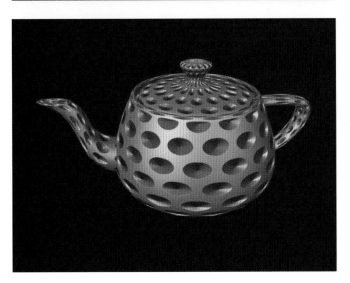

Left and above: **The world-famous Utah teapot, modeled by Newell and rendered by Blinn, was one of the first attempts at creating photographic 3D images on a computer. The teapot can be found in many 3D programs today, and the original piece of crockery takes its rightful place in the Computer History Museum in Utah. Those with an interest can even download the original data for the teapot at ftp://ftp.funet.fi/pub/sci/graphics/packages/objects/teaset.tar.Z**

3D INVADES HOLLYWOOD
Throughout the 1970s and 1980s 3D graphics were a novelty—they tended to be used only by research students, defense departments, and big business. The entertainment industry had yet to find a use for this impressive but geeky technology. However things were about to change.

Thanks to a small group of software developers including Alias Research and Softimage in Toronto, Canada, and Wavefront Technologies in Santa Barbara, California, creating 3D graphics was becoming easier and less technical from a computing point of view. However, while still images were acceptable (for use in mat paintings and industrial visualization) animation was not, at least as far as the use of 3D in movies went.

Disney's *Tron* (1982) was the first major use of 3D graphics in a motion picture, but the movie was a flop despite the huge investment. The problem was the highly stylized look: it lacked realism, partly by design, and partly because 3D technology at that time was not advanced enough. Moviegoers did not approve.

A very simple thing was holding back 3D—motion blur. Fast motion looks blurred when recorded on a movie camera running at 24 frames per second—the camera's shutter is open momentarily to expose a frame of film, but during this time a fast-moving object will change position and hence appear blurred in the frame. The process is similar to the motion blurring that humans experience (because of the persistence of vision effect), and therefore looks completely natural. Without this artifact, as in a series of computer-generated renders, the result is harsh, jittery movement that looks artificial.

For a while, progress seemed stalled while technology caught up. Interest perked up, however, with the work ILM did for James Cameron's 1989 movie, *The Abyss*, where rendered "alien technology" water effects combined seamlessly with actors in the frame. The Cameron/ILM partnership took things one stage further with *Terminator 2: Judgment Day* (1991), in which the liquid alloy body of Robert Patrick's T-1000 villain was recreated digitally, allowing effects by which he could rise from a pool of metal or transform shape at will.

The real breakthrough came in 1993, with *Jurassic Park*. This featured totally photorealistic, computer-generated dinosaurs, perfectly lit, textured, and shaded, and complete with the telltale motion-blur effect. The movie was a massive hit, and its 3D effects work still stands today as some of the best ever produced for a motion picture.

With the appearance of Pixar's *Toy Story* in 1995, the fully CG movie was born. The public acceptance of *A Bug's Life* (1998), *Antz* (1998), *Monsters, Inc.* (2001), *Ice Age* (2002), and *Finding Nemo* (2003) have demonstrated that it's here to stay. And now that no blockbuster—from *The Matrix Reloaded/Revolutions* (2003) to *The Lord of the Rings* (2001-3)—is complete without stunning CG effects, 3D is becoming a crucial part of the language of cinema. In fact, it's getting hard to find a movie that doesn't use CG in some small way.

Below: *Jurassic Park* raised the bar for computer graphics in the movies, and played a key role in placing 3D in the Hollywood frame. For the first time, computer-generated models held their own on the screen with real actors for long periods of the action.
Amblin / Universal / The Kobal Collection

Above: **Pixar/Disney's** *Toy Story* released in 1995, was the first ever all-3D motion picture. Since then there have been numerous 3D classics and this visual approach has taken over from conventional 2D animation as the most popular style in family cartoon movies.

Below left: **Without motion blur 3D animations look awkward and stuttery** —you can see the object clearly in each frame, giving animations a strobelike appearance. In real life, as on film, we expect to see the blurring of fast-moving objects—it's an artifact of the human visual system.

Below: **With motion blur a fast-moving object looks much more realistic.** It's not a trivial thing for a 3D program to simulate motion blur, however, and it took a long time until 3D graphics programs were able to achieve this effect. Now all 3D animation packages worth their salt have it as standard.

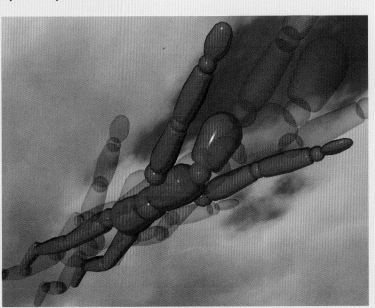

EARLY GAME DESIGN Games have been a fixture of computers almost as long as they have existed. In 1952 A. S. Douglas created a game of Tic-Tac-Toe on the EDSAC (Electronic Delay Storage Automatic Computer) in Cambridge, England, for his doctoral dissertation. Despite the invention of the transistor in 1947, this was still the era of valve-based computers. The huge valve-driven EDSAC had a cathode-ray display tube, making Douglas' program one of the earliest graphical games ever.

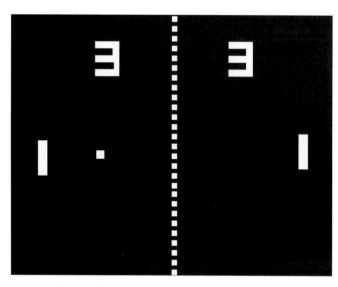

Left: *Pong* was the first hit computer game. It was about as simple as you could imagine but was actually based on a much earlier "game" called *Tennis for Two* created in 1958 Brookhaven National Laboratory, which was played on the lab oscilloscope. *Pong* would eventually become a home console played on a TV set, and it marked the beginning of the home video-game revolution.

As the use of transistors became more prevalent, it was a game that helped demonstrate the power of the new technology in computing. Written for a DEC PDP-1 computer at MIT in 1962, *Spacewar*, the first true interactive computer game, was created by Steve Russell and a team of proto-hackers. Then came games that could be played on a computer connected to a television set, and the ubiquitous games consoles, the most famous of these being *Pong* (as immortalized in the song by Frank Black).

Pong, a simple game similar to tennis, was one of the earliest commercial video games. Installed in clubs, bars, and other public places, *Pong* was a massive hit for the two men who created it: Nolan Bushnell and Ted Dabney, who later went on to form Atari. As it became clear that computer gaming would be a big moneymaker, Atari launched *Pong* as a home console game. The rest is history.

3D games really started in 1980 with *Battlezone*, which used shapes constructed from simple vector lines to represent tanks on a 3D battlefield. The technology was refined with the likes of the *Star Wars* arcade game and *I-Robot*, the first game to include filled-polygon 3D graphics of the sort we would see today. Advances in home computing and the transition to 16-bit processors brought the power to create more advanced 3D games, such as *Starglider* and *Zarch*. With Sega's introduction of *Virtua Racing* and *Virtua Fighting* in the arcades, 3D games were here to stay.

Still, the flat-shaded polygons of those games had little in common with the 3D graphics emerging in other areas. The revolution came with iD software's *Wolfenstein 3D*—a game designed for home PCs. At the time it wasn't believed possible

Below: iD software created *Wolfenstein 3D*, the first 3D computer game. Playable on home PCs, it was a huge leap forward in game graphics technology and spawned many other 3D "shoot-em-up" games.

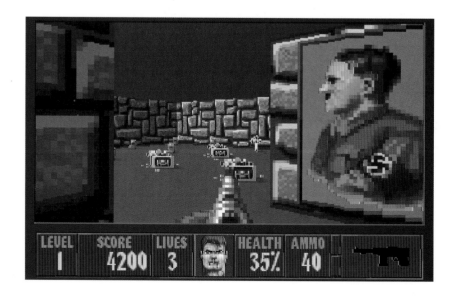

Above left: **As this 2001 remake of** *Wolfenstein 3D* **proves, modern 3D games are incredibly sophisticated, harnessing the power of today's graphics processing.**

Below left: **3D games production is different from 3D for print, video, or the movies. Because of the need for interactivity, game graphics have to balance quality with speed, often requiring highly optimized models and textures to keep CPU overheads as low as possible.**

to create a game in full 3D, complete with texture mapping that would give those plain surfaces a realistic look. A "first-person shoot-em-up," *Wolfenstein 3D* imposed quite a few restrictions in order to create its 3D-rendered graphics—the world could only exist on a single horizontal plane, the player couldn't look up or down, and all objects and characters only existed as flat sprites. Later as CPU power increased, so did the sophistication of the game graphics. iD's next game, *Doom*, added more realistic texture and lighting effects, while the next, *Quake*, included real 3D graphics that could display a more realistic multilevel 3D world inhabited by true 3D characters and objects.

These days game consoles and PCs can display realtime 3D graphics of outstanding realism. As the graphics have improved, the game industry has become larger and more mainstream, making it a hugely profitable entertainment industry on the scale of the music business or the movies.

Computer simulations have been used in engineering and architecture for decades. However, visualization studies of buildings were traditionally done using scale models built of wood, plastic, and foamboard. These allowed the architect to see how the building reacted to light, how it was distributed at different times of day, and whether there were any obvious problems that could be rectified. By inserting cameras into the models, realistic points-of-view could be achieved, giving a fair representation of how the space would eventually look.

When drafting and digital-graphics programs appeared, architects were able to retire their ink pens and french curves and create plans digitally instead. The introduction of digital visualization using 3D graphics revolutionized architecture in the same way as it did engineering. Using a 3D CAD program, architects could turn their plans into 3D models that could be viewed and rotated on screen. In the early days rendering was limited to simple shading of the models, but 3D animations could be created to allow a fly-through of the site from many different perspectives. This also helped the visualization process.

While such simple rendering techniques helped architects to see the form of the buildings, it did little to convey the way light would illuminate the building, at least with any accuracy. Luckily, the introduction of more sophisticated rendering techniques changed that. Modern 3D programs can now render buildings using techniques such as radiosity (*see page 100*) which models better the way ambient light bounces around a scene, while accurate texture mapping

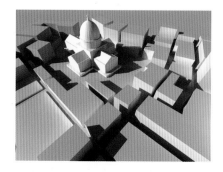
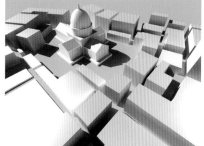
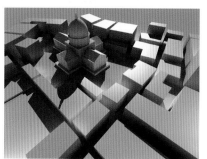
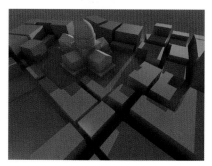
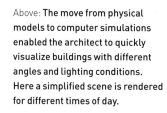

Above: **The move from physical models to computer simulations enabled the architect to quickly visualize buildings with different angles and lighting conditions. Here a simplified scene is rendered for different times of day.**

Left: **Using modern 3D rendering techniques such as radiosity and global illumination, architects can perform sophisticated lighting studies of interiors and exteriors.**

also improved the rendered image, producing something that was much more recognizable as a digital prototype of the finished building.

All this is especially helpful when pre-approving plans with clients, because they get a new photographic idea of what their building will actually look like with the materials specified. They can see interiors and exteriors from a variety of angles and under different lighting conditions. To make things easier, we now have architecture-oriented 3D rendering programs, in which the architect can specify lights using more familiar units, such as the Lumen, Candela, etc., rather than some arbitrary number.

LOW-END 3D

In the early 1990s professional 3D design was done using powerful workstations and software costing thousands of dollars. As the market for 3D products was small and R&D was costly, the expense of these programs was only to be expected. Typical 3D programs, such as Softimage | 3D, Wavefront Technologies' Advanced Visualizer System, and Alias from Alias Research, were all designed to run on high-cost UNIX computers from the likes of Sun and SGI.

As 3D progressed, the technology began to trickle down into cheaper 3D systems designed for desktop PCs and Macs. Some of these early programs included Lightwave (originally called Videoscape 3D), which was designed as a 3D utility for Newtek's Video Toaster digital video system, running on the now defunct Commodore Amiga. Another was 3D Studio, a DOS program for PCs (later to become 3ds max).

There's still a thriving low-end 3D market, because not everyone needs or wants professional features and the complexity they introduce to a program. Over the years the low end has seen many and varied 3D programs and plug-ins: some have lasted the test of time, many have not. If all you need is to texture map a few spheres, or lathe a curve to make a vase, then there are simple plug-ins that can add 3D to existing 2D graphics packages. Adobe Dimensions is a good example, although it has not been updated for several years. Another plug-in for Adobe Illustrator is 3D PopArt from Vertigo. This program is about as simple as it gets, allowing you to convert any path in Illustrator into a 3D object.

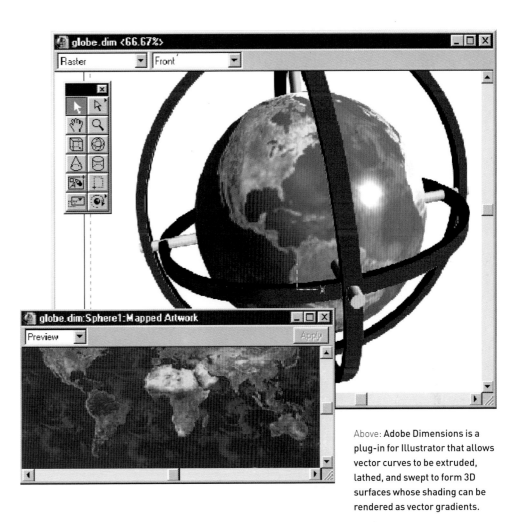

Above: **Adobe Dimensions is a plug-in for Illustrator that allows vector curves to be extruded, lathed, and swept to form 3D surfaces whose shading can be rendered as vector gradients.**

Right: **Bryce is a landscape-generation package that has a long and fruitful history. Bryce images are often easy to spot since they usually feature craggy mountains, infinite oceans, and candy-colored skies, but it's also possible to create some exciting 3D images using the program.**

01.02

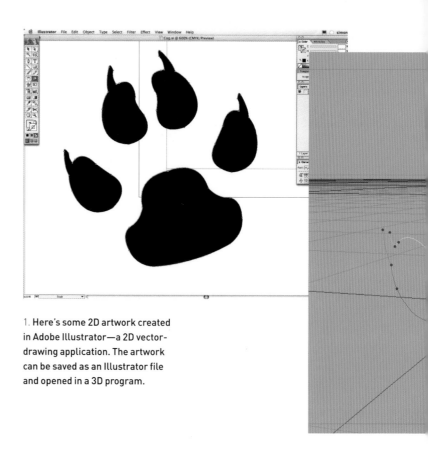

1. Here's some 2D artwork created in Adobe Illustrator—a 2D vector-drawing application. The artwork can be saved as an Illustrator file and opened in a 3D program.

3D PRESENT

2D-3D WORKFLOW Although 2D and 3D design are quite different disciplines there is a symbiotic relationship between them. 3D artists will often use 2D design tools in their workflow while occasionally a 2D artist will make use of a 3D tool. Although the latter relationship is optional, the former is essential.

Adobe Photoshop is the most popular 2D image-manipulation tool used in 3D design. Photoshop will be used during the production of a 3D-rendered image and after, for touch-ups, color correction, and compositing if needed. Other useful 2D tools include the lower-cost JASC Paint Shop Pro, Corel Photo-Paint, or GIMP (a free, open-source UNIX/LINUX application). There are also some dedicated 2D paint programs designed specifically for 3D artists. These include Maxon's BodyPaint and Right Hemisphere's DeepPaint 3D. These two are designed primarily to tackle the problems faced by 3D artists in creating textures that fit around 3D objects without smearing, but they have image manipulation and compositing tools.

So 2D paint programs—known as bitmap editors because they work with pixel-based images—are integral to the 3D workflow for creating and editing texture maps and for retouching renders. However vector-drawing programs, such as Adobe Illustrator and Macromedia Freehand, can also serve a useful role. Most 3D programs can import Illustrator format files or the cross-platform .EPS file format and then convert the vector curves they contain into 3D spline curves. These can then be used as sources for additional modeling procedures.

Let's see how this works in a typical workflow. Imagine a client wants a 3D artist to produce a rendered animation of their company logo. This is supplied to the artist as an .EPS file. The artist opens the .EPS directly in the 3D program and extrudes the curves of the logo to create a 3D version of it with thickness. The 3D object is animated and rendered and the result delivered back to the client. The client is happy and the 3D artist gets paid.

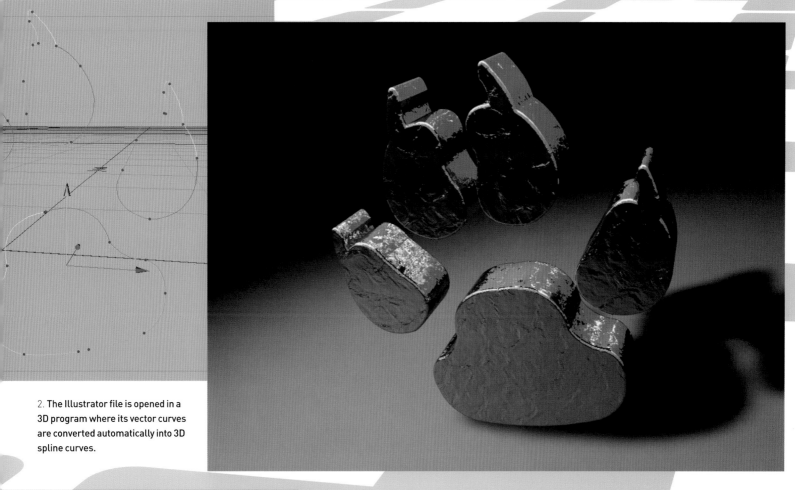

2. The Illustrator file is opened in a 3D program where its vector curves are converted automatically into 3D spline curves.

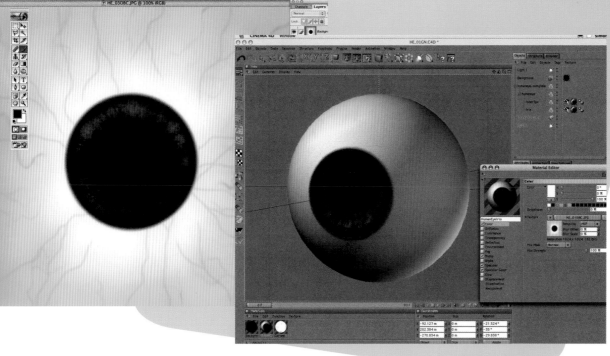

3. These curves can then be extruded to create a solid 3D object that matches the original 2D artwork. Its surface can be given a material and rendered.

Left to right: **2D paint programs,** such as the ever-popular Photoshop, form an integral part of the 3D workflow. Here Photoshop is used to create a texture of an eyeball, which is then used as the texture map on the 3D object.

chapter 02. 3D present

THE BIG 6 The 3D market has been a volatile one over the last few years. On the one hand, the technology has expanded hugely. On the other, prices for advanced 3D packages have come down drastically. Currently the 3D market exists on several plateaus, from the basic—and low-cost—starter package to the full-featured, high-end application suite.

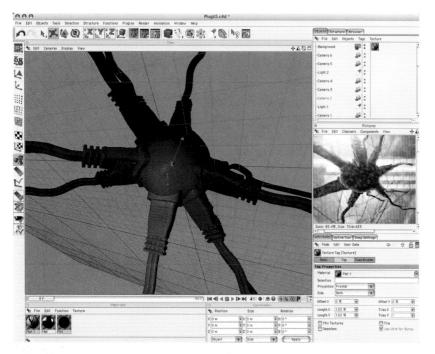

On the bottom end of the market are the basic 3D applications—low in price and simple to use, suitable for home users or those wanting quick and dirty 3D without having to pay an arm and a leg or spend ages learning a complex program.

Mid-range programs offer many features that a few years ago were considered state of the art, such as dynamics simulation and powerful rendering and animation facilities, but at the reasonable price of the average 2D graphics program. Some specialized 3D programs in this market tackle specific 3D problems, such as getting 3D on the Web, animating human figures, or creating 3D environments.

At the top of the market are the high-end 3D programs used by professional 3D designers and the big animation studios (who may also use their own custom 3D tools). Currently there are six major 3D packages that anyone interested in pursuing 3D should know about.

At the very top is Side Effects Software's Houdini range: an incredibly powerful set of applications, but perhaps too complicated for the non-technically minded. Next are Alias Maya Unlimited and Softimage | XSI Advanced, both of which are fully featured 3D systems incorporating hair and fur rendering and the cloth simulation needed to create advanced 3D characters. Both companies also produce cheaper versions—Maya Complete, and XSI Foundation or Essentials—which have some of the more advanced features removed.

Left above: **Maxon Computer's Cinema 4D** is a very powerful yet friendly high-end 3D system that many 2D artists will find easy to get to grips with.

Left below: **Lightwave 3D** has a long heritage, first appearing on the Amiga platform. It's famous for its rendering engine, which is one of the very best at any price.

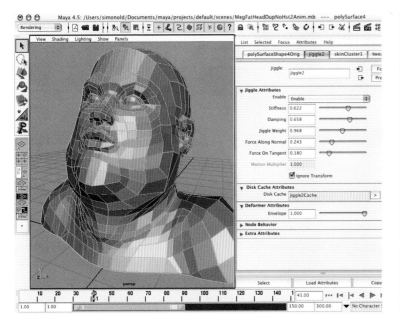

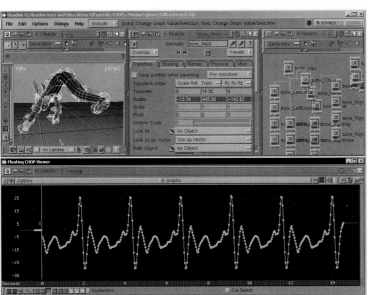

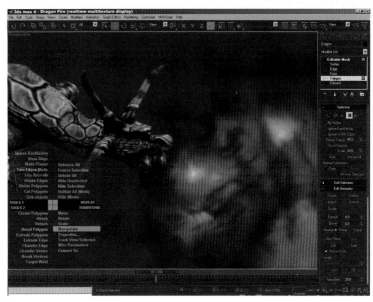

In the middle pricewise is Discreet's 3ds max. It's an all-round 3D system and also rather complex to use, but it has become the favored tool for 3D game production. Lower down in terms of price and ease of use, though certainly not in capability, we find Maxon's Cinema 4D and Newtek's Lightwave 3D. The latter is especially popular for broadcast television graphics. All these packages can produce top-flight 3D work: the artist using the tools makes the real difference.

Augmenting the high-end 3D packages are numerous plug-ins and rendering tools. The most notable is Pixar's photorealistic Renderman software. The rendering toolset alone costs as much as the more expensive 3D animation packages, but is favored by many special effect studios as their rendering system of choice.

Above left: **Maya has quickly become** the industry-standard 3D package, but it's not without its detractors. It comes in two versions: Maya Complete and the more expensive Maya Unlimited.

Bottom left:**The Houdini suite of 3D** tools from Side Effects use a clever procedural design system. This is not for the faint of heart, but it offers clear advantages for high-end production.

Above right: **Softimage | XSI is a very** powerful and elegantly designed 3D system. It's now offered in three versions, Foundation, Essentials, and Advanced.

Bottom right: **3ds max from Discreet** is a powerful integrated 3D system. The package has become one of the most popular 3D applications in the computer games industry.

THE FUTURE Attempting to predict the future of any kind of technology is difficult, let alone within the fast-moving area of 3D computer graphics. All the same, there are some trends that can be extrapolated, and these enable us to make reasonable assumptions about what we might expect in the future.

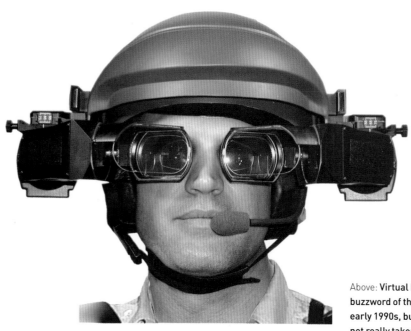

Professional 3D programs will continue to become more complex as new features and technology are developed. On the plus side, these technical improvements mean that the creations of 3D artists will become ever more incredible, but this trend still causes problems for developers and users. For the user of a 3D program, easy workflow is hindered as complexity increases, while for developers it becomes a struggle to maintain ease of use in a 3D program as the feature count increases. There comes a point in an application's development where the focus shifts from adding more and more features (which are often requested by users) to an overhaul of the workflow and interface and a rationalization of tools and commands.

And that's not all. Numerous companies are working on the next generation of 3D applications, and these will hopefully make the current methods look antiquated and cumbersome. Luxology has already demonstrated their next-generation 3D modeling program called Modo, which goes some way toward clearing away the clutter of current 3D toolsets in favor of a more fluid and simple workflow. In the area of character animation, game giant SEGA is developing a 3D system that looks very promising. Called Animanium, it uses 2D cel-animation techniques and a simple interface, which requires no training to use, according to SEGA.

Above: **Virtual Reality was the buzzword of the late 1980s and early 1990s, but the concept has not really taken off, at least for consumers. The promise that we would all be communicating in a virtual 3D environment by the 21st century was an empty one and—with hindsight—a silly one, given the size and cost of the hardware.**

At the bottom of the market we can expect to see the trickle-down effect continue, where technologies that were once state of the art become commonplace and affordable to consumers and hobbyists.

It's a sure bet that 3D will continue to be used in entertainment, advertising, architecture, and engineering. What is not clear is whether 3D graphics and virtual-reality systems will have any role in our everyday lives in the future. It's possible that 3D computer interfaces will become commonplace, and that 3D programs will be as ubiquitous as word-processing applications. It's also an exciting thought that at some point computers will be so powerful that we will no longer need to wait for photorealistic rendered images to be computed.

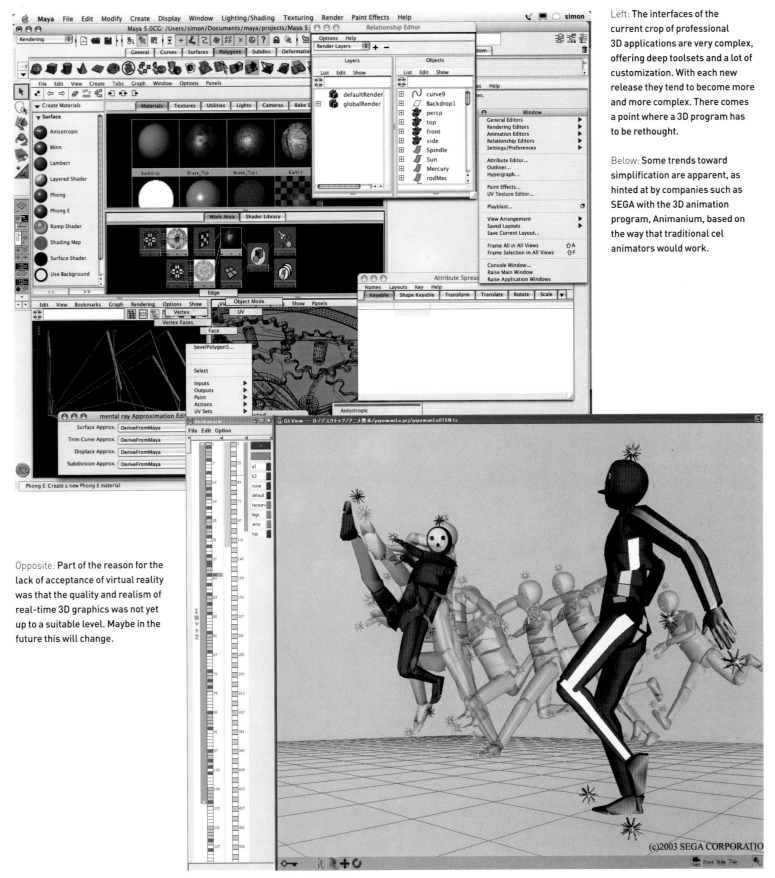

Left: The interfaces of the current crop of professional 3D applications are very complex, offering deep toolsets and a lot of customization. With each new release they tend to become more and more complex. There comes a point where a 3D program has to be rethought.

Below: Some trends toward simplification are apparent, as hinted at by companies such as SEGA with the 3D animation program, Animanium, based on the way that traditional cel animators would work.

Opposite: Part of the reason for the lack of acceptance of virtual reality was that the quality and realism of real-time 3D graphics was not yet up to a suitable level. Maybe in the future this will change.

(c)2003 SEGA CORPORATIO

3D IN THE REAL WORLD

02.01

3D AT WORK

3D VISUALIZATION An area in which 3D graphics has proved invaluable is in previsualization. With 3D graphics you can create images of products yet to be manufactured, buildings that have only been planned, and engineering projects yet to get the go-ahead. And that's just the tip of the iceberg: there are the automotive, aerospace, and biomedical industries, too. 3D is also used in chemical processing, hurricane analysis, and other scientific disciplines. Although not necessarily creative, these demonstrate the far-reaching uses of modern 3D technology.

However as a modern graphics tool, 3D imagery has really revolutionized creative design and visualization. In the past, product designs were initially sketched, ideas tossed around and discussed, then detailed plans and drawings skillfully and painstakingly created by hand. Although it's still difficult to capture the immediacy of a pencil-and-paper sketch produced just as inspiration strikes, the rest of this process can be transferred to the computer.

The process begins by creating a 3D model, reproducing the geometry of the real-world product. Then materials can be defined for the object's components, and finally the scene can be lit and the shot composed. A 3D camera can then capture the scene, rendering it at any size, angle, and quality as often as required. A 3D image can be viewed from any angle—there's no need to redo anything as you would with a hand-drawn image, and if changes need to be made, that can likewise be accomplished. Perhaps the gadget needs to be longer, redder, or made from a different kind of plastic. Perhaps you want to see it in different settings or against different backgrounds. In any case, it takes a lot less time to produce these changes with 3D software than it would by hand, and you get a better feel for the final object.

Left: This is a 3D visualization of a perfume bottle for an advertising campaign. The bottle has been placed on a virtual set and rendered as if it had been a practical model that was photographed.

Below left: Here's the scene displayed interactively in the 3D program used to create it. It's possible to change anything in the scene—the lighting, the camera angle, even the materials—in a matter of minutes.

Opposite: It's just as easy to create an entirely new setting for a product, such as in this image. The change took a few minutes—much easier and less expensive than a shoot in an exotic location.

Below: In this image the scene has been re-rendered, but this time the camera used simulates a depth-of-field blurring to focus attention on the product rather than on the background. This is a subtle change, but it makes a big difference.

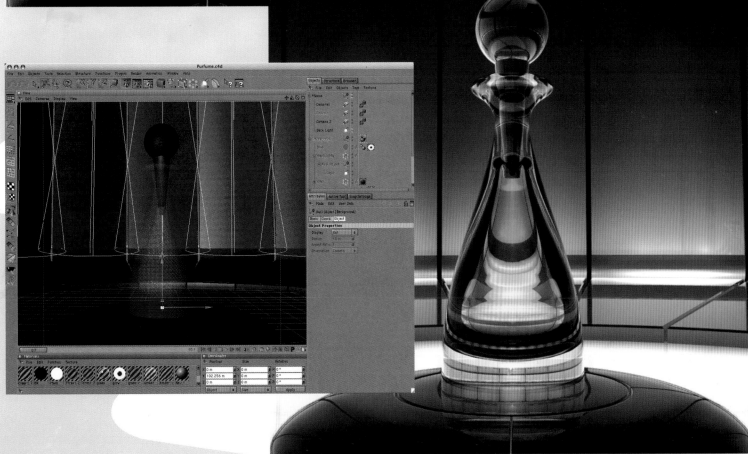

chapter 01. 3D at work

CAD AND PROTOTYPING

Creating an image on a computer is one thing, but eventually a product has to be manufactured. The skill of a product designer is being able to transfer concepts and ideas into products that can actually be built. 3D visualization offers designers the ability to analyze the structural integrity of a model using specialized computer-aided design (CAD) tools.

Engineering aspects, such as structural stresses, fatigue, and aerodynamics can all be analyzed using sophisticated CAD software, which can help to ameliorate any shortcomings in the original design.

Computer-aided manufacturing is the second stage of the process. The CAD model data can be used by the computer-controlled machine tools in a manufacturing plant to cut, mill, lathe, or form materials into the desired shape. In this way a real object is generated from the 3D ideal: the manufacturing equivalent of Platonic idealism.

Another way to generate a real object from a 3D model is by stereolithography. This is a process that uses a computer-controlled laser to curve a special resin, layer by layer, to create the 3D form. Just about any CAD file can be used in this process, which is known as rapid prototyping. There are companies that specialize in rapid prototyping services; you send them a 3D model file and they create the resin prototype. Rapid prototyping offers a very quick way to refine a product, because it allows you to perform visual inspection and fit-and-finish tests on a real object. While the resin model cannot be used directly, it can be used to create a mold for the final object.

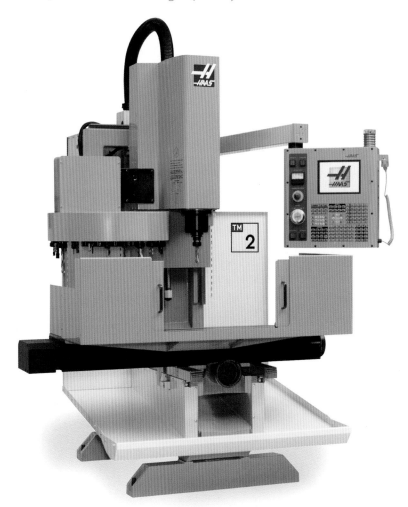

Above: **Computer-aided manufacturing involves the use of 3D (or 2D) data created on a computer to control a machine tool. This is a typical CNC machine by Haas used for milling complex shapes from metal.**

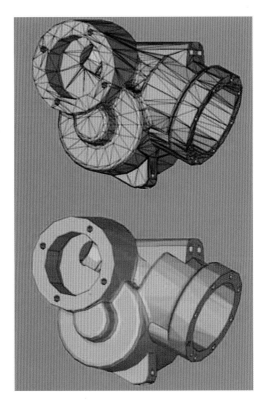

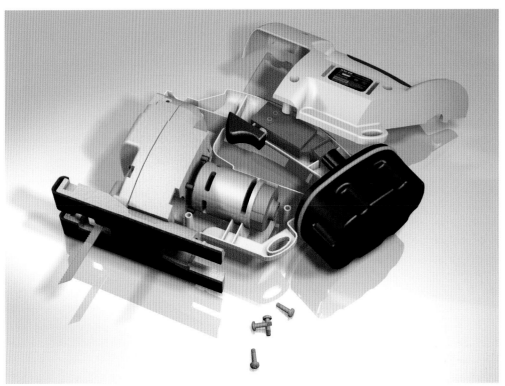

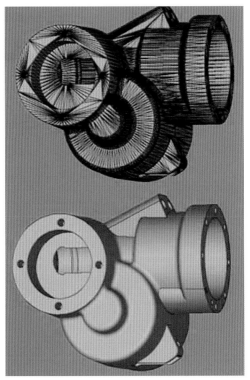

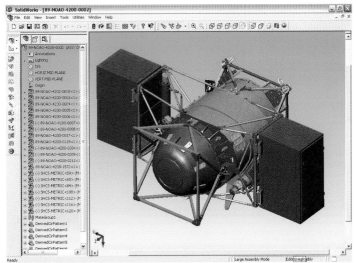

Left: The standard file format for stereolithography, .STL, stores the object's geometry as a set of triangular facets, which define its outer and/or inner surface. The .STL file can be imported and manipulated in 3D and industrial CAD applications, provided they have the right converters.

Above: CAD and Mechanical design applications, such as SolidWorks, go beyond object modeling and animation to component assembly and stress analysis. With CAD and CAM applications, photorealism isn't as vital as clarity, accuracy, and the ease and speed of use.

3D SIMULATION, 3D VIEWING, AND VR

Simulation is another application for 3D graphics, and because it is often generated in real-time, it has a lot in common with game production. You can simulate just about anything in 3D so its field of application is very broad. Some of the more common uses for 3D simulators include aviation and aircraft training, medical imaging, and, of course, entertainment applications such as theme park rides.

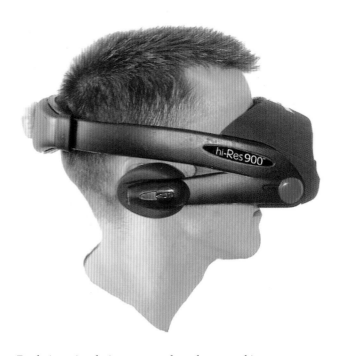

Real-time simulation systems have been used in many situations, from scientific research to games and entertainment. Virtual reality is an offshoot that combines real-time 3D graphics with 3D goggles or some other device to create the impression of a real environment enveloping the user. Many attempts have been made at creating viable virtual-reality systems, but it seems that it has not caught on, at least for most of us. But 3D VR systems still tend to be expensive, and so their application is limited. As a way to interface humans and computers, 3D has not yet been successfully exploited and, although a nice idea, it may be that VR is not the right approach.

3D shutter glasses can be used for viewing videos and DVDs filmed with stereoscopic cameras. These are relatively inexpensive but the film libraries are not that extensive. A stereoscopic camera films the action from two slightly separated lenses (corresponding to the positions of our two eyes). These two images are combined into fields in a single video frame and play concurrently. Televisions display each field alternately at 60hz (60 times a second) and the shutter glasses block each eye at the same frequency using liquid crystal lenses. In this way, the left eye receives only the left image and the right eye only the right image. This can cause annoying flickering, so a technique called vertical sync doubling is often used, which effectively doubles the rate at which images are displayed, reducing the effect.

Such systems can be used to view 3D-rendered animations that have been stereoscopically rendered. This is not a difficult process to achieve, and in fact any 3D animation package can generate the images required for stereoscopic 3D. It's just the way the two images are combined that enables them to be viewed using shutter glasses. A motion-graphics application such as Adobe After Effects can also be used for this, using the field interlacing options.

3D shutter glasses are also used for viewing 3D games in true 3D. The glasses connect to the video card in the computer, and because computer monitors can usually display at much higher frequencies than a TV set, vertical sync-doubling is not usually required.

Left: Virtual-reality systems attempt to simulate an immersive environment with which the user can interact. Goggle-based VR systems were typically bulky and uncomfortable to use for long periods, but the technology is steadily slimming down.

Below: Many 3D accelerator cards enable you to connect LCD shutter glasses for playing 3D games in true 3D. With monitors capable of changing images at rates of 100Hz or more, these systems are quite comfortable to use.

HAPTIC FEEDBACK

3D is used extensively in medical research and training, but one of the problems with 3D graphics is that you can't interact with them physically. However, engineers have devised a way around that problem using haptic feedback systems. These provide physical simulation that correlates with the visual simulation on screen to form the basis of surgical training devices.

Flight simulators also combine haptic feedback and 3D graphics but on quite a different scale. Trainee military and passenger jet pilots spend hundreds of hours in industrial flight simulators which are exact replicas of the cockpits of commercial and military jet planes. The windows are replaced by computer screens displaying the simulated 3D scenery. The cockpit is mounted in a special hydraulic rig that can move the entire system in all axes to give the impression of real flight—turbulence included.

The converse of the use of haptics in simulation is its use in the 3D creation process itself. At one time 3D modeling was often done by plotting the positions of points on the surfaces of a clay model, particularly for organic objects that were difficult to create in 3D directly. It was easy for model builders to make a maquette or sculpture in clay and then digitize it using a sensor pen attached to a computer by a series of jointed arms. These systems have since fallen out of favor partly due to their expense but also due to new photographic 3D digitizing techniques.

The probe concept can be used instead as part of a haptic control system. Such a system lets 3D artists sculpt models using an arm-pen probe. They then receive feedback through the probe, giving the sensation of sculpting a real object.

Above: **A flight simulator combines realistic 3D graphics with real movement used for training jet pilots. These expensive systems utilize powerful computers and mimic the characteristics of commercial and military jet planes.**

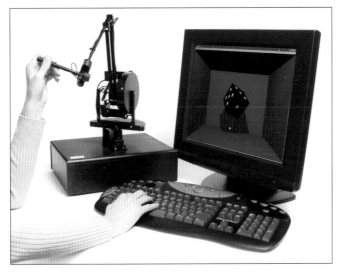

Right: **Phantom is a haptic input device (also known as a force-feedback device) produced by Sensable Technologies. It provides tactile feedback to users of 3D software as they sculpt and manipulate 3D objects.**

ARCHITECTURE Architecture is a design discipline that deals directly with 3D forms, so 3D graphics fits perfectly with it both as a design and visualization tool. It has also become a way for architects to explore flights of fancy more dramatically than ever before.

Copyright (c) 2003 Chen Qingfeng(Xiamen,China

Many architects design on the computer, although they may not enter the 3D modeling stage immediately. Ideas may be sketched and worked up in plan form initally, but it's also possible to work directly with 3D software right from the beginning. It's just a matter of individual preference. However, this is a fairly recent development. Traditionally, 3D models were only created once the design and planning was set, since making changes to a 3D model as complex as an entire building would be time-consuming and costly. Modern 3D architectural software offers more creative freedom than ever before. With fast modeling tools and real-time display rendering, architects are allowed to explore their ideas directly in 3D.

These days the focus is more on efficiency and productivity, with programs making use of referencing, instances, and procedural models to help to fill in the details of a building (such as prebuilt windows and doors with customizable parameters that can be dragged and dropped into place).

One program of note is called SketchUp by AtLast software. It is designed to be an architect's 3D sketchbook: a program that has the speed and directness of pencil and paper but the power and flexibility of a 3D program. It features smart cursors that detect angles and intersections as you build in 3D.

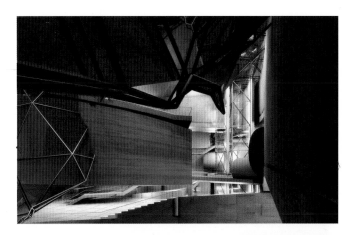

Opposite: **Using powerful radiosity rendering techniques, highly accurate lighting simulations can be performed in the computer. These beautiful examples by Chen Qingfeng demonstrate the subtle skill of setting up and rendering impressive lighting simulations in 3D.**

Above right: **Using 3D software, architects can explore many different aspects of their buildings, including materials and lighting.**

Right: **This image shows the masses of detail that would typically go into creating a building in 3D. If there are many repeating structures in a model, they can be created using instances—a feature that may come in useful if the architect needs to be able to alter them later. A small part of the building that is repeated hundreds of times can be changed by editing the master object; all the instances update automatically.**

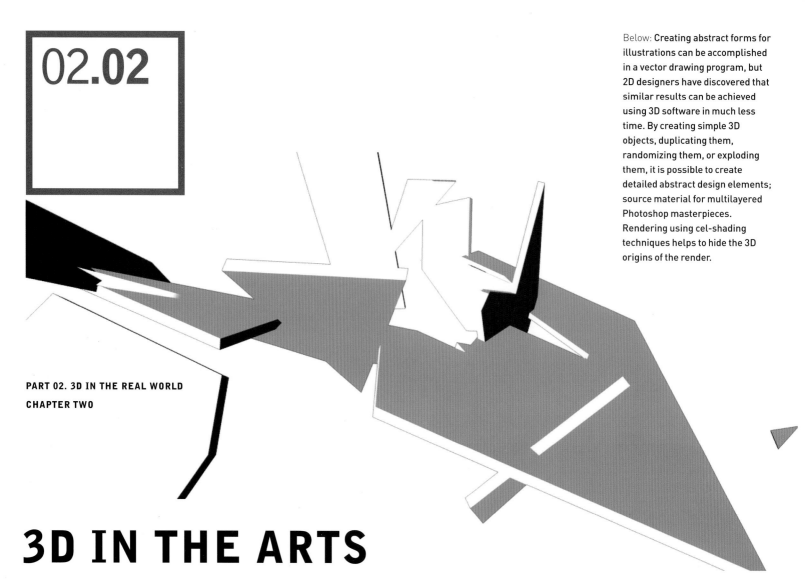

PART 02. 3D IN THE REAL WORLD

CHAPTER TWO

Below: **Creating abstract forms for illustrations can be accomplished in a vector drawing program, but 2D designers have discovered that similar results can be achieved using 3D software in much less time. By creating simple 3D objects, duplicating them, randomizing them, or exploding them, it is possible to create detailed abstract design elements; source material for multilayered Photoshop masterpieces. Rendering using cel-shading techniques helps to hide the 3D origins of the render.**

3D IN THE ARTS

DESIGNING IN 3D FOR 2D It may not be immediately apparent that 3D can be a useful tool for the 2D artist working in print or on the Web. However, non-photorealistic rendering techniques mean that 3D software can work in tandem with illustration and image-editing programs to create great 2D artwork.

A recent trend has been toward the use of abstract 3D forms in digital illustration. By combining vector and Photoshop artwork with complex abstract 3D forms, contemporary illustrators have forged a new direction that merges traditional and cutting-edge techniques. 3D programs have played a crucial role in this modern style, becoming a trusted tool in the creative design toolbox.

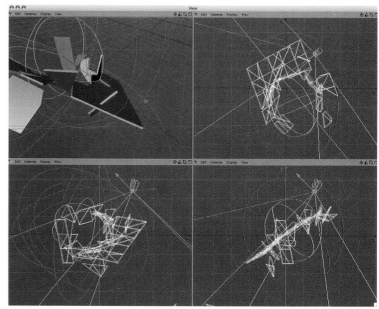

Right: The ability to manipulate perspective in 3D offers a wide range of creative possibilities, too. The computer keeps the perspective correct, even when it is greatly exaggerated.

Below left: 3D can also be used conspicuously for illustration work, but by keeping detail and clutter low and using simple objects and plain surfaces, designers can create cool illustrations that seem half 2D, half 3D.

Below right: Again by avoiding photorealistic pitfalls, designers make 3D applications ideal tools for clean-cut illustration work. Even when using techniques like raytraced reflections, unnatural shapes and structure can prevent images from losing that abstract quality.

Above: **A typical low-polygon game character. Note that most of the detail comes from the texture map applied to the model. The model is "light," geometrically speaking, so it can be rendered interactively.**

Right: **Game developers need to keep polygon counts to a minimum in order to keep the graphics flowing. A 3D tree can be made using two mutually perpendicular triangular polygons. Mapping a tree texture onto each gives a fair impression of a 3D tree that can be viewed from most angles. This is the color texture.**

Far right: **And this is the alpha channel used to stencil out the tree image from its background.**

3D GAME DESIGN Computer gaming has become a significant part of modern culture, and it's an area in which 3D rules supreme. Early computer games date back almost as far as the computer itself, but it wasn't until the introduction of color graphics that games really began to enthrall kids and adults. When the first 3D games appeared they were really revolutionary, while the games of today are nothing short of astounding.

3D game production is an involved process. It's quite unlike any of the other creative uses for 3D graphics because of the simple fact that game graphics are generated in real-time. In movie and video production, illustration, or visualization, the final rendered image is produced slowly, because the rendered image needs to be high quality and that takes time. For 3D games the definition of "quality" is different entirely. It's all about the playability of the game and the speed of the graphics rather than photorealism, and in order to achieve this compromises have to be made elsewhere.

One compromise is to make 3D models with a lower polygon count. That means that the geometry used to create the game scenery and characters is as simple as possible while still having enough detail to be visually interesting. Texture maps are used to make up for the lack of detail in a game model, and this explains the typically "blocky" look of game characters.

The 3D graphics you see on-screen while playing a game are rendered interactively, at rates of 30 frames a second or more, yet a typical high-resolution frame for a

motion picture might take three minutes to render. That's a mere 0.056 frames per second. 3D game graphics need to be generated 540 times faster on average than film and broadcast graphics, which puts things into perspective.

While games developers can make use of hardware acceleration and special rendering software such as OpenGL or DirectX, they still need to be efficient in the use of geometry, textures, and lighting in order to achieve fast frame rates. Developers often use clever tricks and sleight of hand in order to imply detail that is not actually there. However, as computer hardware is become more powerful, games are becoming richer and more detailed. The current crop of 3D games are incredibly so, featuring real-time reflection maps, detailed models, volumetric effects, and more.

Below: **When applied to the two polygons you get a fairly decent-looking tree.**

SPECIAL EFFECTS

Arguably the most demanding, visible, and visually impressive use of 3D graphics is in effects for film. The applications in this field cover just about every possible use for the technology. In fact movie special-effect production is one of the most potent driving forces in the development of 3D applications. Such vital advances as realistic simulated hair, fur, and cloth have all been developed primarily because film production demands them.

Left: **One area that 3D has yet to conquer is that of the digital actor —the "Synthespian." While 3D animated creatures, monsters, or cartoon characters have been accepted, it's more difficult to create realistic humans, with all their foibles, complex emotion, and behavior. The best attempt so far was made by Columbia Pictures and Square Pictures Inc. with the cutting-edge, all-3D movie** *Final Fantasy: The Spirits Within* **(2001).**

Below left: **Desktop 3D applications make it possible for independent artists to create animated movies. Chris Bailey's short** *Major Damage* **was created by a core team of three with assistance from 3D artists worldwide.** Major Damage TM © Copyright 2001 Chris Bailey. All rights reserved.

3D graphics are used to create digital landscapes, seascapes, and scenery, to modify or remove existing buildings, or even re-create ancient ones. 3D graphics are also commonly used to create explosions, laser bolts, digital planets, and space scenes, and such effects are now within the budget of even modest movie and TV productions. There are hundreds of 3D studios around the world working on countless movies, and the 3D production industry is set to get even more prolific.

As well as the effects you see on screen, 3D is used as a preproduction tool, too. 3D animated storyboards, known as animatics, are common on big Hollywood productions, and these can be used to work out camera angles and ascertain any difficulties that might occur when shooting real footage that is to be combined with 3D imagery.

Below: Merging live-action footage and 3D graphics seamlessly is essential for creating today's blockbuster special effects. It's rare for an entire shot to be 100 per cent 3D, even in the most intense battle scene. The best 3D work on the big screen, as in *The Lord of the Rings: Return of the King*, comes when live action is combined with digital effects, but the process isn't simple. Matching the lighting, the look, and the tone of the movie, plus the movement of the camera, requires the skills of large numbers of talented 3D artists.

DYNAMICS 3D programs have come into their own in the field of producing effects and digital trickery for TV broadcast and movie productions. One area in which 3D programs have improved in recent years is dynamics simulation.

By integrating physical laws and behavior in 3D programs, developers have enabled 3D artists to create animations that include realistic natural motion. Objects fall as they should under the influence of gravity, rigid bodies collide, shatter, and scatter as they should in real life, and soft bodies deform as they should during movement.

In 3D, animation is usually done by setting keyframes for various parameters on an object—its position, rotation, or color, and so on. For large scenes involving characters or machines with many moving parts, even a simple animation can be a complex business. If you want to throw your character down a flight of stairs, or cause two speeding vehicles to crash, animating by hand is going to be a laborious and painstaking process.

Using dynamics algorithms you let the computer take over and calculate the effects of collisions, gravity, and other physical forces for you. These rigid-body simulations can be calculated and converted to keyframes (in a process known as "baking") so that the calculation only needs to be done once. Like rendering, a physical simulation can require some time to be processed, so converting to keyframes lets the simulation be played back in real time. Having the simulation baked also means it can be edited if necessary using the 3D program's keyframe-editing tool set.

A good example of rigid-body dynamics can be seen in the pod racing scene from *Star Wars Episode I: The Phantom Menace* (1999). In this scene Maya was used to crash several highly detailed pod-racer models, and to calculate the vast number of parts that

Above: **Using rigid body dynamics, you can set up a collision and let the software calculate the myriad interactions that occur as a result. Such an animation would be next to impossible to create any other way.**

broke off and flew from the tumbling pod-racer engines. The great results speak volumes for the use of dynamics simulation in effects work.

Softbody dynamics is a separate branch of dynamics simulation in which forces and collisions cause the surface of objects to deform. Softbody simulation can be used to animate objects and surfaces that were tricky to do properly before, including water dynamics, cloth, and fabric, rubber, and the motion of the human body. For the latter, softbody simulation provides a way to add "jiggle" and bounce at a stroke. This secondary motion (motion that occurs in reaction to the primary movement and which may continue after it has stopped) is essential for the creation of believable characters, especially if they are large, bulky, and carry a lot of excess flesh.

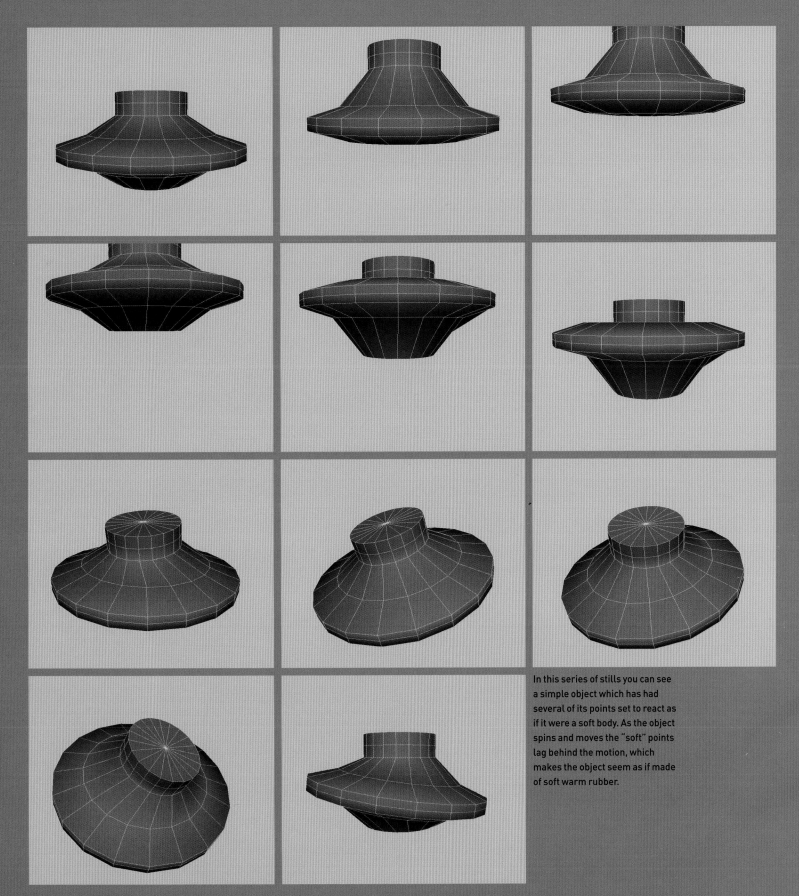

In this series of stills you can see a simple object which has had several of its points set to react as if it were a soft body. As the object spins and moves the "soft" points lag behind the motion, which makes the object seem as if made of soft warm rubber.

BROADCAST GRAPHICS

BROADCAST GRAPHICS In the world of broadcast media, 3D has become essential for creating titles and graphics for programs and live events. It seems that no sports coverage is complete without some spinning, glittery, animated graphic or a flashy 3D scorecard.

3D now has a place in nearly every kind of program, from quick visualizations in sports programs to animated characters in children's shows. The downside of the popularity of 3D graphics and animation in broadcast media is that some visual styles quickly become hackneyed. Luckily, traditional flying logos and shiny spinning letters are slowly being replaced by a more subtle merging of 2D and motion graphics with 3D elements that doesn't scream CGI at you. It is a sure sign that audiences are becoming increasingly accustomed to the use of 3D and that their taste for it is becoming more sophisticated. The pressure is on for ever better graphics and animations.

Left: Traditional flying logos can be easily created in any 3D program. For broadcasting they need to be rendered at the native resolution and frame rate of the broadcast medium. In the US the NTSC format has a resolution of 704 x 480 pixels and runs at 30 frames per second. The PAL format used in UK and most of Europe has a slightly higher 720 x 576 pixel resolution, but runs at a slower 25 frames per second.

Left: 3D animations destined for the TV must also be rendered to take account of the fields of the broadcasting systems. Television systems don't display whole frames one after another; rather they display them using a process called interlacing. First the even rows of pixels are displayed, then the odd rows. Since each odd and even row is shown alternately at 50Hz (NTSC) you effectively double the frame rate, albeit at technically half the resolution. Because of the persistence of vision phenomenon and the speed of the scan rate, we don't register this flickering of the image between odd and even fields. A video still containing moving objects will show the fields clearly, however. When rendering in 3D you can usually save fields rather than whole frames.

Left: 3D characters can be found hosting TV programs, in commercials, and channel identifiers and often in children's television programs. Simple 3D characters are ideal for children's TV, continuing the trend set by traditional cel-animation.

Left: Graphs and charts are a typical subject for 3D news graphics. With bold colors, clean lines, and animation, statistical information can be given an interesting visual makeover.

3D DIGITAL VIDEO EFFECTS DVEs (Digital Video Effects) give motion graphics artists and video editors a huge range of creative possibilities when it comes to designing broadcasting visuals. Most motion-graphics and video-editing programs come with a 3D plug-in of some description, which lets you wrap video images around 3D surfaces, perform sophisticated 3D transformations, and layer video clips in new and imaginative ways.

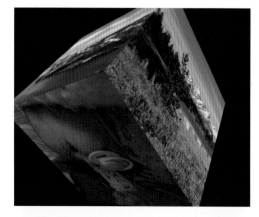

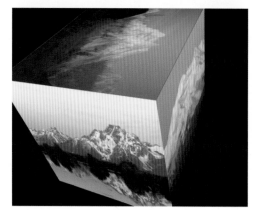

Moving up a level, motion-graphics programs such as Adobe After Effects, Discreet Combustion, and Apple Shake now integrate near-full 3D environments in what is still technically a 2D domain. These programs offer varying degrees of 3D freedom—some even have lights and cameras like a 3D program. These are usually more difficult to work with in 3D however, which is why 3D programs make ideal complementary tools for DVE work.

Above: **Using a video clip instead of a still image means you can perform sophisticated DVEs in a 3D program. A classic example is the video cube. Each face of this cube has a different video clip assigned to it. During the animation the cube spins, playing the video clips as it does so.**

 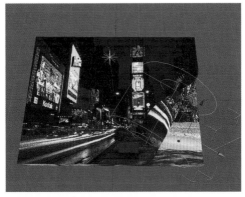 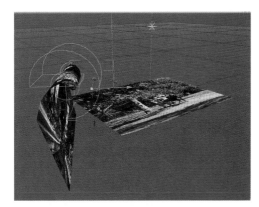

Above left to right: **Another classic DVE** is the page curl. Although it has been overused (to say the least) it's a good effect to demonstrate how DVEs are done in a 3D package. In this example a page curl is used to to make the transition between one clip and another. Two planes are positioned one on top of the other, and an ambient light is added to the scene and set to 100 per cent so that the video planes display without any shading.

A bend deformer is applied to the topmost plane, which is heavily subdivided, with a bend angle of 270°. As the bend deformer is moved across the scene, it curls up the plane revealing the one below.

The reason the bend is 270° is so that the bent plane does not become visible when it curls over. If a 180° or 360° bend is used then the plane will become visible again as the bend passes though it. With a 270° bend the excess part of the plane travels vertically downward through the plane at the bottom.

Above: **By rendering from a non-perspective top view,** the effect appears seamless. You could animate the bend at any speed, or change its angle and direction to create variations of the same effect. This is just the tip of the iceberg, of course—the sky is the limit with 3D DVEs.

WEB 3D It's usually only 3D artists and gamers who get to experience interactive 3D graphics. Displaying rich 3D content on a computer can be demanding on system hardware, which is one reason why 3D graphics on the Web have taken a while to become established. Another is that, generally speaking, the data required to render a moderate 3D scene is quite large. However, this is changing. The proliferation of broadband Internet access means that rich Web content, including large graphics, animation, and 3D on the Web is a reality for many users.

There are many different Web technologies and standards in use on the Web, with numerous companies supplying their own brand of 3D content deployment, compression, and display software. There are a few different schemes involved but the one that is emerging as favorite is where a Web browser plug-in renders and displays the raw 3D data that is downloaded. This allows maximum compression of the data while in transit, and most of the hard work of creating the 3D scene is handled on the fly at the receiver's computer.

However, Web 3D graphics still seem to be limited to certain markets and genres, and typical Web users may have never even come across a site containing interactive 3D. If they do, they will most likely have to download a plug-in of viewer, just as if they wanted to view a site enabled with Shockwave or Flash. Thankfully many of these viewers have reduced in size from one or two megabytes to a few hundred kilobytes, making installation a pretty painless process, even through a dial-up connection.

Two popular Web 3D technologies include Viewpoint VET and Shockwave 3D. In order to create Shockwave or Viewpoint 3D content you need to install an export plug-in for your particular 3D application. Most of the big 3D apps are supported, so it's relatively simple to create scenes and deploy them on your site.

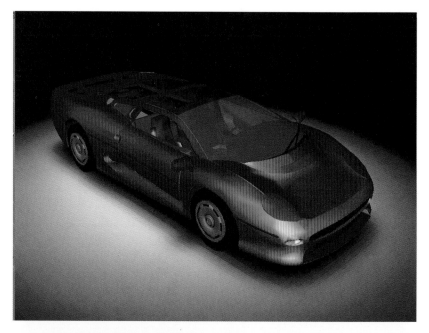

Above right: **Cortona is a VRML-based Web 3D system by Parallel Graphics.** Users can download the viewer for free to view 3D-enabled websites. There are many different developers and technologies for using 3D on the Web, so if you come across a site using a different system you may need to download a specific 3D viewer.

Right: **When viewing Web 3D content, you generally have a** screen in a Webpage, which you can manipulate by dragging. The controls offered differ depending on what has been implemented for that scene and what is supported by the 3D system itself. You will usually be able to rotate, pan, and zoom the view as a minimum.

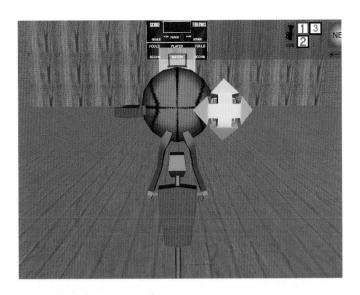

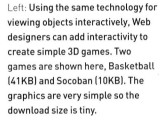

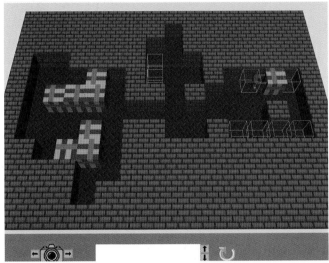

Left: Using the same technology for viewing objects interactively, Web designers can add interactivity to create simple 3D games. Two games are shown here, Basketball (41KB) and Socoban (10KB). The graphics are very simple so the download size is tiny.

Right: By taking photographs of real locations and using them as texture maps on simple geometry, you can create virtual environments based on real locations. This, for example, is Montmartre in Paris, France.

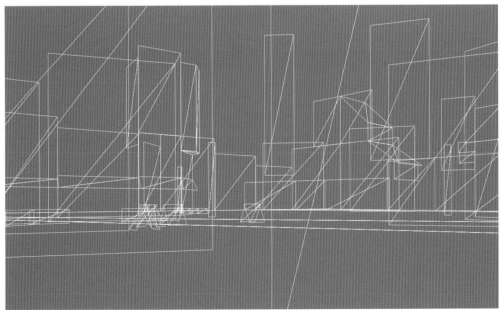

Left: The geometry of this scene is extremely simple, and at only 4.2KB it represents a near instant download. It's the textures that take longer, but with careful preparation even these can be reduced to a mere 600KB or so.

2D TO 3D

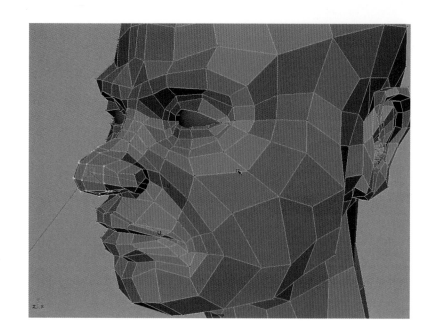

2D CANVAS AND 3D SPACE

Getting to grips with working in 3D can be difficult, especially if you are used to the 2D canvas offered in traditional painting and drawing applications. With 2D art, what you see is what you get: you are directly creating the final image as you work in Adobe Photoshop, Illustrator, or whatever program takes your fancy. In 3D the workflow is quite different. You begin by building the elements that make up the final artwork (or animation) but the actual image itself doesn't come together until quite late in the process. Therefore, working on a 3D scene takes a certain degree of planning and forethought: otherwise you can waste a lot of time working on parts that ultimately contribute little to the final image.

The other big difference between 2D and 3D workflows is that the tools are more abstract in 3D than in a 2D program. In Photoshop, say, you have tools that correspond directly to the finished artwork—a brush, a pen, a clone tool, etc. They are all used to work on the final image itself so there is a logical relationship and directness between the tools and the artwork. In 3D the tools can seem bizarre, awkward, or nonsensical, and they don't always relate to the finished image in any way. It is this very sense of being at one remove from the artwork that many 2D artists struggle with when they first migrate to 3D.

However, it's something that you do get used to, like moving a pointer with a mouse while you're looking at a computer screen. 3D artists are always thinking ahead—imagining how what they are currently working on will work in the finished scene—and this is a skill that can be learned with practice.

The other problem 2D artists face is how to transfer from a flat world of two dimensions to the infinite void of three. Thankfully most 3D work is done on flat planes, too, even when working in a full 3D environment.

Opposite: Painting on a 2D canvas is simple because you are using a 2D input device (a mouse or pen) to control 2D tools. But when you watch a 3D artist working on a model in a 3D-perspective view, it can be difficult to grasp what's going on. While it may seem that work is being done in three dimensions, that's usually not the case.

Right: If a 3D artist decides to move a point on a 3D model, he first selects it. Handles are displayed that indicate the three axes of movement, X, Y, and Z, and by dragging one handle at a time the movement of the point is constrained to that single direction.

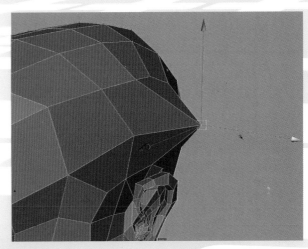

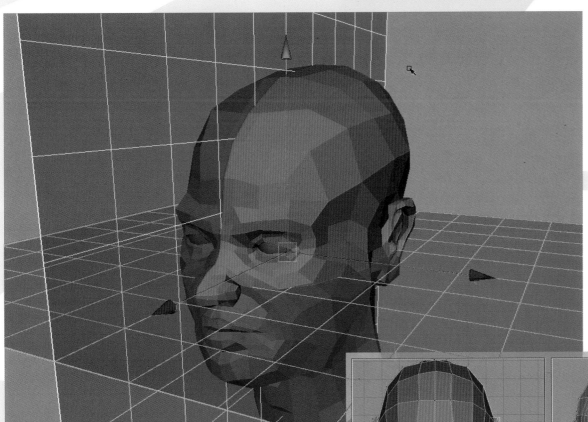

Left: While an artist may be viewing or rotating a model in 3D, the actual work of modeling is often done in one or two dimensions at a time. This is because it is impossible to use a 2D input device such as a mouse or graphics tablet to input 3D data accurately. By using a set of axes to control the movement of points, polygons, or objects, the 3D artists can limit the movement either to a plane or along a specific axis, despite viewing the scene in 3D. Models are usually built facing a particular axis so they are correctly aligned to begin with.

Right: By rotating the view around after each edit, you can more easily tell where in 3D space the point is and adjust its position one axis at a time. Alternatively, viewing three orthogonal views at once shows you the position of the point along the three axes, which makes correct positioning very easy.

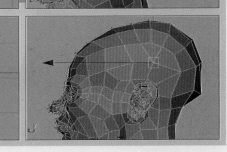

PERSPECTIVE Until about 1400 AD perspective was poorly understood. Prior to this, some attempts were made at re-creating its effects but the rules governing it proved hard to grasp. The earliest perspective paintings had lines converging at different points in the distance, causing objects to look distorted. They still worked as artistic images, but technically speaking they were incorrect.

A 3D program can generate accurate perspective automatically without your having to work it out, but it still helps to understand the principle of perspective and how it can be created in 2D. Thinking about every aspect of a design including those that the computer calculates for you, can be beneficial in terms of the clarity of your design.

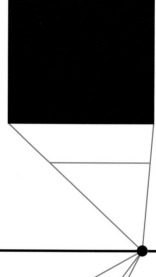

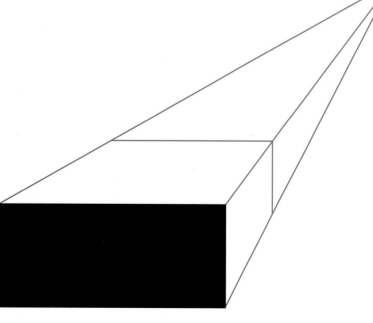

Above: **Simple perspective can be calculated by defining a vanishing point and extending all straight lines to this one point. The vanishing point is the point on the horizon where it appears that parallel lines converge. Of course they don't really converge—it's just the effect of objects shrinking in size as they get farther from us. You can draw straight-sided objects using this method, but it's not totally accurate as only one set of parallel edges of a cube is used to generate the perspective; the other lines remain parallel in the drawing. One-point perspective generates objects that have one side facing directly toward us.**

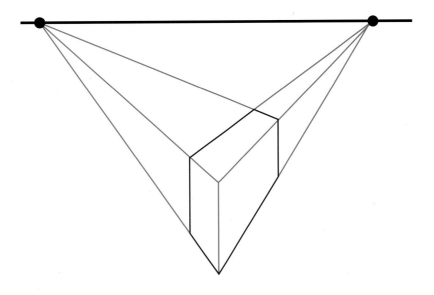

Left: Two-point perspective is created by using two sets of parallel lines on a cube or block. It can be used to create objects that are not directly facing the viewer. Instead of a single vanishing point, two are chosen, and corresponding edges are extended to these points of reference. The closer together these points, the more dramatic the perspective.

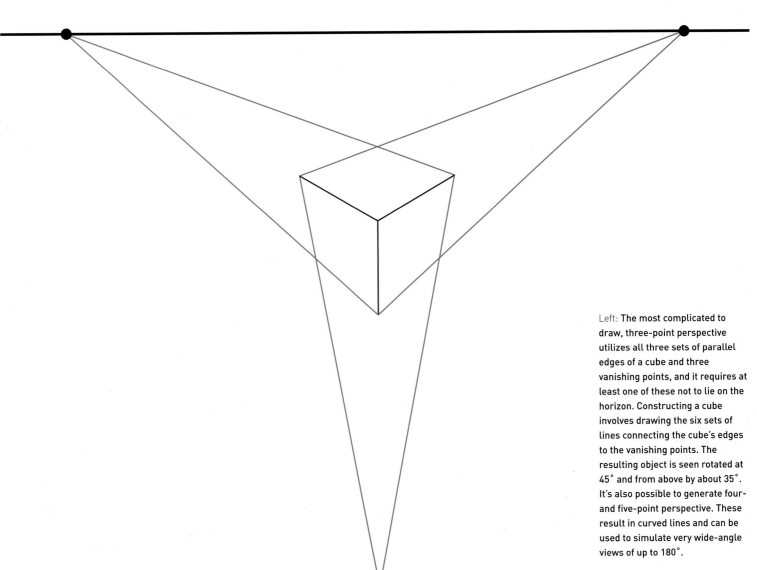

Left: The most complicated to draw, three-point perspective utilizes all three sets of parallel edges of a cube and three vanishing points, and it requires at least one of these not to lie on the horizon. Constructing a cube involves drawing the six sets of lines connecting the cube's edges to the vanishing points. The resulting object is seen rotated at 45˚ and from above by about 35˚. It's also possible to generate four- and five-point perspective. These result in curved lines and can be used to simulate very wide-angle views of up to 180˚.

SIMULATING 3D IN 2D Despite the power, flexibility, and complexity of 3D programs, it's still possible to do great 3D work in a 2D program. After all, painters have been creating realistic pseudo-3D images for centuries using tools far less sophisticated than the average 2D image-editor. By taking the behavior of light, materials, surfaces, and perspective into account, you can easily create near-photoreal results in Adobe Photoshop alone.

This example is a humorous image created entirely in Photoshop. It makes use of techniques and analysis that would also be done in a 3D program to achieve realism, but it maintains a 2D style all of its own.

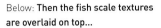
Below: Then the fish scale textures are overlaid on top...

Bottom: Finally shading is applied, taking into account that a fish is partially translucent. Note that you get the impression of a backbone through the skin, and that the body, which is less obscured by bones, is bright orange because more light can pass. The head which has thicker bone, is a red-orange color. Interestingly, these are the same things you would bear in mind if you tried to create the same image in a 3D program.

Above: You don't need a raytracer to create glass reflections. The glass bowl sports two large window reflections that are simple 2D shapes overlaid on the image. Subtle use of masking provides Fresnel fall-off for the reflected shapes just as it would in a 3D render. Remove the reflections, and the glass bowl instantly looks fake.

Above right: The effects of light play a big part in determining the look of an object's surface. Translucency is the key to getting the fish to look right, and all it needs is some time with a digital paintbrush. The fish begins its life as a flat shape.

Below right: Then some color is added...

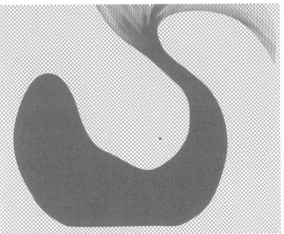

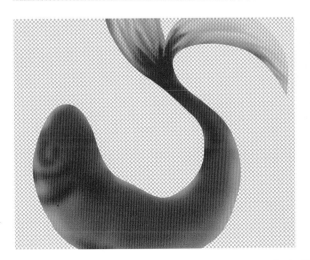

SPATIAL AWARENESS AND DESIGNING IN 3D Spatial awareness is important for the creation of realistic 3D images. Being able to rotate, transform, and dissect forms in your imagination is essential for drawing figures and objects correctly, no matter what environment they are created in. In some ways this ability is more important for 2D artists than 3D artists, because as long as you are methodical, the computer will always maintain the spatial relationships of objects when working in a 3D program.

Drawing on a 2D canvas can be more demanding because you have to build spatial information into your image by hand, often working out complex perspective solutions as you go. Some artists just have a feel for it, and whether in 2D or 3D their work always looks good.

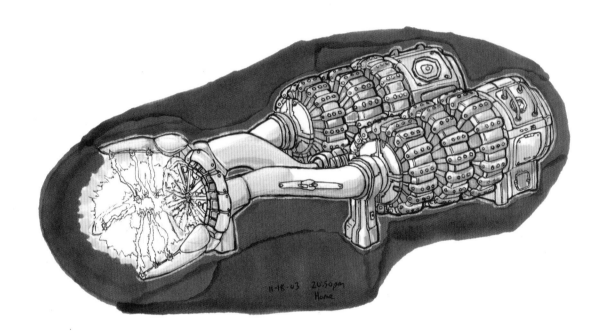

Above right: **Spatial awareness is also crucial when designing a 3D object. The idea may start in your head but it'll often still require some sketching before the proportions and the relationships between parts of the model look good. Here's a sketch of a plasma-cannon design created by Brian Pace.**

Right: **Once the design is sketched a model can begin to be built in 3D. It doesn't always have to be done like this, since some 3D artists can sketch directly in 3D, but a pen and paper is usually quicker for trying design ideas out. Next is an image of a simplified version of the model in 3D. The key design elements are in place and the overall form and proportion looks good. Unlike a 2D sketch the 3D design can be rotated and viewed from all angles—this will help to show up any weak areas of the model.**

Opposite top: **Once the design is settled, the 3D artist can work on the model until the desired level of detail is achieved, adding textures and lighting for a final render.**

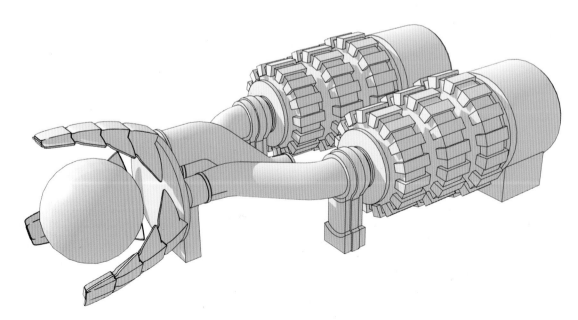

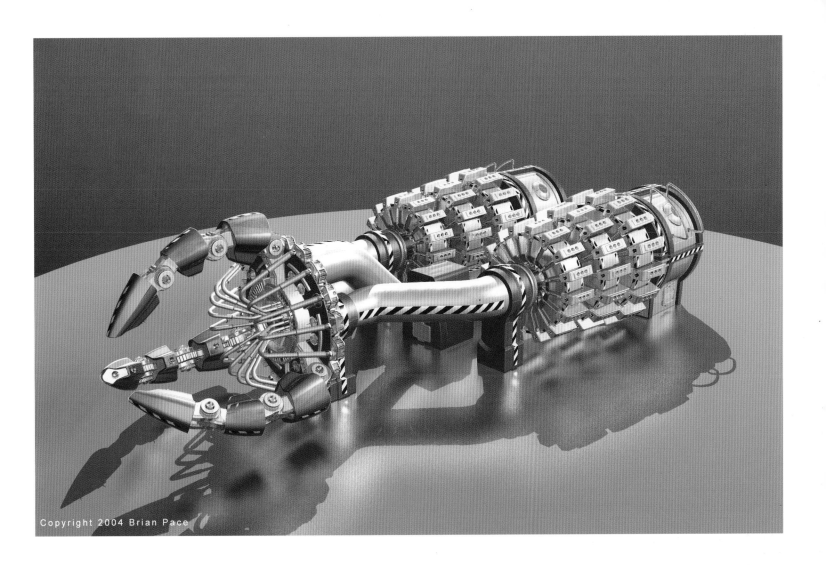

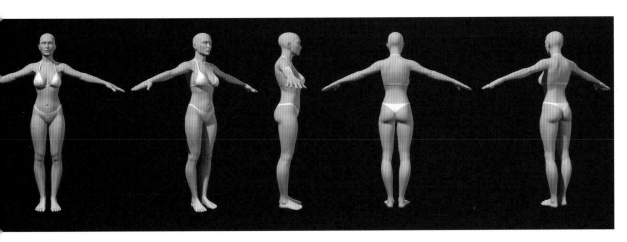

Left: When building 3D models, especially very complicated ones like human characters, 3D artists will rotate the object using a shaded view so that they can grasp the form of the object in their mind. The computer monitor only displays a 2D image so this constant rotation back and forth helps to make the object a little more three-dimensional. It's as if the artist is holding the object and turning it around to look at it from all sides.
Dan Phillips, http://dcp.lihp.com

RE-CREATING PHOTOREALITY A lot of 3D work involves realism. The term you'll often hear used is "photorealistic" when discussing such work. There's a difference between photorealism and plain old realism, and that has a lot to do both with the way 3D programs are designed and the ultimate use of the 3D images.

3D programs are designed around the concept of the camera. Because much 3D work is intended either to match images already photographed or replace them (such as in visual effects or visualization) the photo aspect of photorealism is key to achieving seamless and believable results.

When a camera takes an image, it captures light by focusing it onto a photographic film or light-sensitive CCD chip. It's a similar system to our eyesight, but one that's not quite as well designed or sophisticated. As a result the camera/lens system is prone to many kinds of visual quirks and artifacts, and simulating these is often key to achieving photorealistic results in 3D. However, it can require lots of effort to get these artifacts to work convincingly in a scene.

One quirk is to do with the way that the lens of a camera focuses—a quality known as depth of field. When the lens aperture is opened up wide (particularly in low-light situations), the focal distance is reduced. Objects closer to and farther from the point of sharp focus appear blurred. When focusing on a subject very close to the camera, this depth of field blurring can be very pronounced. In fact, some modern photographic techniques involve tilting the film plane relative to the lens to achieve an even more pronounced, artificial depth blurring.

Left above: **Depth-of-field blurring is an artistic device that you can make use of in 3D work. If you want to emulate close-up macro photography, making use of the depth-of-field feature in most 3D programs can give your renders that photoreal quality. Without DOF rendering this image is fine, but it lacks realism. The fact that everything is in sharp focus actually makes it oddly confusing.**

Left: **By enabling DOF rendering and setting up the camera so that the butterfly is at the point of perfect focus, the render is much more realistic. It's also a more pleasing composition, because the busy background has been blurred.**

Above: Another artifact is lens flare. This occurs when bright light enters the lens at a shallow angle and causes obscuring reflections within the lens system. Photographers try to avoid this by using lens hoods to prevent stray light from entering the lens, but it can also be used creatively.

Left: In 3D, lens flare can be simulated. It is usually defined per light as opposed to per camera. This allows you to control exactly which light is to produce a flare. A great effect is produced when an object passes in front of a light that has a flare, causing the flare to cut in and out. This adds a tremendous amount to certain 3D animations —if used sparingly.

SHADOWS AND LIGHT Light and shadow play an important role in any image, whether generated in a computer, created by hand, or photographed. Because you have to position and set up lights as if they were real objects when creating a 3D image, it is important to understand the roles that light and shade play in an image, or you risk getting carried away by the technicalities of the lighting rig itself.

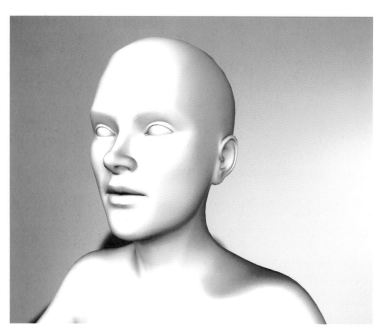

It's very easy to get 3D lighting wrong. It can take a lot of trial and error to get to grips with designing a 3D lighting rig, making it easy to overlook the artistic impact light can have. It's interesting to note that, by and large, 2D artists begin with a white canvas and add shading to it to create objects and images. A 3D environment is totally black to begin with and the process is reversed—in a sense you are adding darkness to the image. As you add lights, you define areas of illumination as opposed to areas of shadow. This is where many novices make their mistake—it's all too easy to over-illuminate.

It's not necessary to illuminate the whole surface of an object; this is especially true for animations. The object has to be readable, and for that, well-defined edges are essential. When you sketch with a pencil and paper, you generally start with edges and add the shading. Even a rough sketch can read very well with well-chosen lines and shading. The same approach can be taken with 3D.

Opposite, top left: **This image has too much illumination. There are** only two lights used but they have washed out the image, resulting in very little shading and a lack of tonal balance in the image. The shadows are not well placed either. There's very little interest in the image because the lighting gives everything away and does not show the object off well.

Opposite, top right: **This image is more interesting. The lighting is** almost nonexistent, with two lights as before, but this time one is a very low-value fill, the other a bright light positioned behind and to the side so that only a sliver of light catches her face. The artist is not attempting to illuminate the surface of the model at all, but trying to show the edges. However, only one side of the model is delineated. How can we do the same to the other side without making her brighter?

Opposite, bottom: **Simple. Add** another light but shine it on the background only. Now the side of the model not illuminated has been delineated as a silhouette against the brighter background. Using a spotlight, it is relatively easy to aim the illumination so that none is cast behind the bright side of her head. One side is black against white, the other white against black.

Below: **The same technique can work well for multiple subjects. In** this example, one character is lit brightly against a black background while the other is in shadow against a light background. The lighting can be reversed to suggest a different mood or change the emphasis between the subjects.

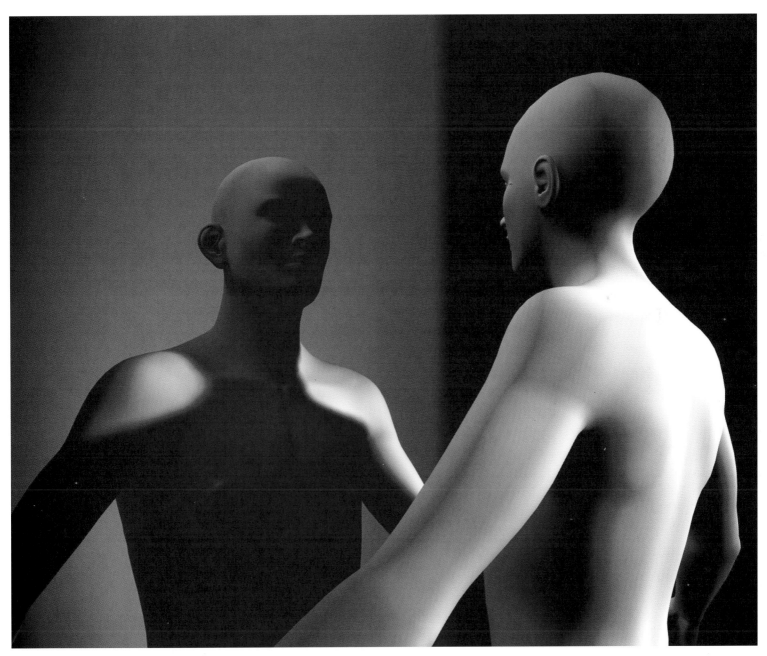

3D CORE CONCEPTS

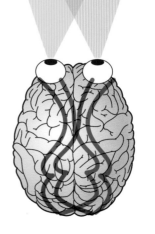

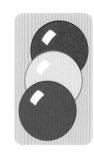

PART 04. 3D CORE CONCEPTS

CHAPTER ONE

THE NATURE OF 3D

At the most fundamental level, digital 3D graphics offer a visual simulation of the physical world in which we live. Although they are sometimes confused with the term "virtual reality," they are not the same thing. However, this link with reality is important. Once you break down the core of what makes 3D graphics tick, you come to understand the ways in which 3D graphics relate to reality.

Currently digital 3D graphics are used intensively in a limited number of fields, including the entertainment industry, engineering and design, architecture, and even the world of fine art. Their use in virtual reality systems has so far been limited, simply because it's still not possible to create truly believable, fully immersive graphics at the display rate required—in real time. Affordable computers aren't powerful enough yet. However 3D technology and computing power are slowly eroding this barrier, and it is conceivable that in the future 3D graphics will play a greater role in our lives.

This may actually have important moral and philosophical implications in the future, as digital 3D becomes ever more proficient at simulating reality. We are already at the stage when 3D artists can create still images that are indistinguishable from photographs, and these artists can do so in very little time. Of course, the image created by 3D software is a 2D image, but the same goes for the image formed on our retina by the lens of our eye. It's only our stereoscopic vision that adds the sense of depth. Perhaps technology in the future will let us feed digital 2D digital images directly into our brain, or scan them directly onto our corneas. How easy will it be for us to tell if what we are looking at is real or generated?

Above: **We see because light is focused by our corneas, at the front of the eyes, onto the back to form a 2D image. We see in 3D because our eyes take in the scene from slightly different viewpoints. Our brain reconciles the two eye images in a single 3D image.**

Left: As digital 3D increases in its ability to capture the subtle nuances of reality, it's getting harder and harder to tell the difference between what's real and what is computer generated, as this image shows. There's no evidence to suggest this trend will cease, and in the future it may be impossible to tell what is real and what isn't.

Above: *Mousetrapped* by Studio 3D. (www.studio3D.com). By rendering the same scene from slightly different positions, it's possible to create left- and right-eye image pairs digitally. The tricky part is feeding one image to one eye only, and the other image to the other eye only. Research is taking place into creating true stereoscopic 3D displays without the need for 3D glasses, but it's still a long way from becoming a practical reality. Instead, we use glasses to filter the image. One method uses glasses with polarizing lenses, which alternately become opaque then transparent, connected to a display that alternates between the right and left image in time with the glasses. Do this quickly enough and the result is a 3D image.

COORDINATE SYSTEMS To make sense of a 3D world, your computer and its 3D applications rely on one very simple principle, that of a coordinate system. Just as a 2D map relies on latitude and longitude to define a location, so in 3D space you need a set of coordinates for your computer to know where any given point is. In 3D graphics, the Cartesian coordinate system is used, named after its inventor, the mathematician and philosopher René Descartes (1596–1650).

Descartes realized, watching a fly one day, that he could describe its position at any given point in time by a series of three numbers. Each number would describe the fly's position along one of three mutually perpendicular fixed axes.

The three axes, X, Y, and Z, all meet at their zero point—called the origin—and from this central location extend away in a total of six directions; X,-X, Y,-Y, Z,-Z. Using Cartesian coordinates we can write the origin as 0,0,0, with some other random location in space relative to it as 23,-5,10, or another as 200,100, -100, or 5.78,300.3,29847.23. The magnitude of the values is unrestricted since the axes extend infinitely.

Once you have a coordinate system in place you can define points in space. Create two points and join them, and you have a line; add another point (not on the line) and you have a triangle. The triangle is important in 3D graphics because it represents the simplest shape possible. Triangles have another important property—they cannot be bent. If you try to bend a triangle you'll only rotate it in space. No matter how hard you try the three points will always lie on a plane.

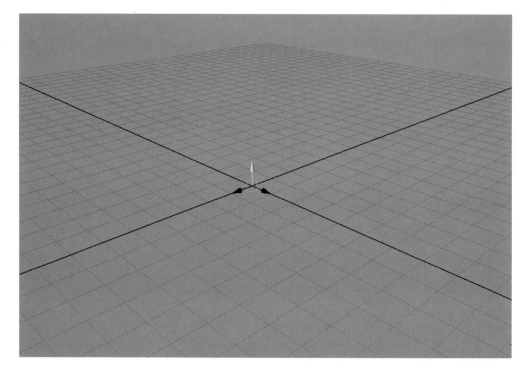

Above: **In all 3D programs you will find a grid and a set of axes. Most of the time, the 3D scene you create will be located at the origin, because when you create a new 3D document, the 3D program will place the origin at the center of the screen. It makes it a lot easier starting from 0,0,0 than from some other random point in space.**

Right: **A triangle consists of three points connected together by lines (also known as edges). The triangle is the simplest shape in 3D and for that reason it's important because other more complicated shapes can be built from it.**

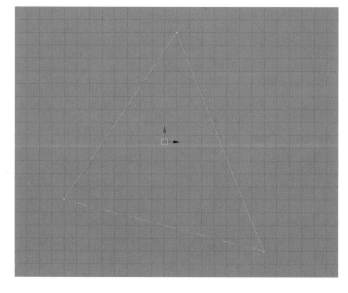

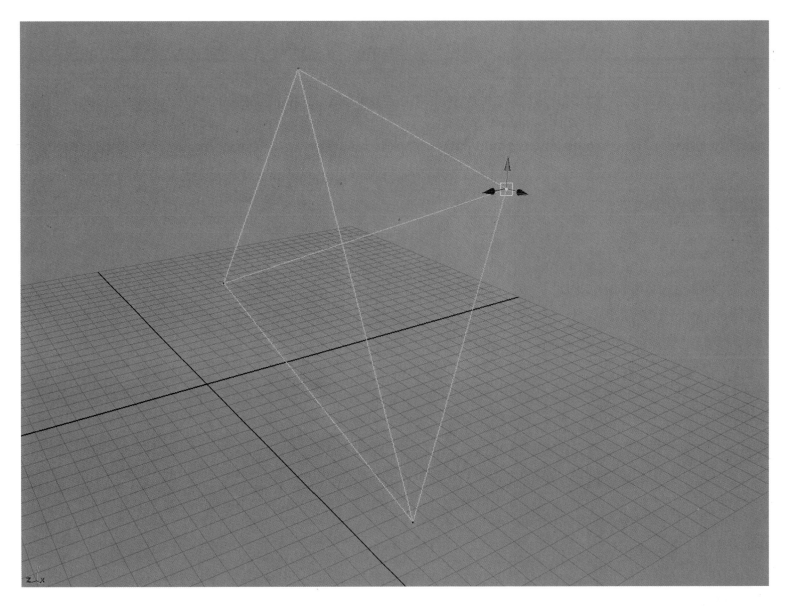

With a coordinate system you can define points, with points you can define shapes, and with shapes you can make objects. Everything in 3D graphics is dependent on the coordinate system, and this is a very important concept to remember.

Now, let's move to the next logical level to see how we can make three-dimensional objects. If we take our triangle shape and add another point that does not lie on the same plane, and join the other three points to it with edges, we have the simplest 3D solid object, the tetrahedron. By creating many points and joining them to form a net of triangles, we can create just about any surface shape we like. This is the essence of making models on a computer.

Above: **Adding a fourth point to our triangle, making sure it does not lie on the same plane, gives us a tetrahedron. The tetrahedron is made up of four triangles sharing a total of six edges. This is important. An object in 3D is only "solid" if the flat shapes that make up its surface are connected so that they share common edges.**

Right: **More complex objects are made in the same manner, but the number of points, edges, and triangles is increased. A torus is displayed here with shading.**

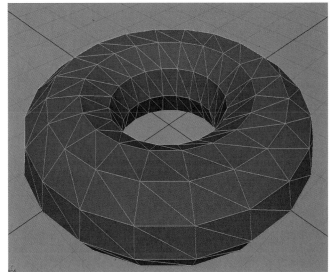

THE VIRTUAL 3D ENVIRONMENT With the theory of coordinates in place we need some way to make it work for us. In the early days, the only way to create 3D objects was constructing them point by point by typing in strings of numbers. Luckily, modern computer and operating systems let 3D-graphics developers create elegant 3D programs, with GUIs (Graphics User Interfaces) that are friendly enough for artists (rather than just programmers) to use.

A typical 3D program features a large 3D view pane surrounded by tool buttons and menus plus panels containing information about the scene and its parameters.

Most 3D programs are based around a simple theme, that of tools and views. The application usually has a main 3D view, with numerous tools and panels that provide feedback and information about what is going on in the scene.

The 3D window usually takes up a large portion of the interface, because most 3D graphics work is interactive. That means 3D artists can literally get their hands on their 3D models to move, rotate, scale, edit, and extend them as they build their scene or object. The view panel can display different types of views, too, and often more than one at a time. The most common arrangement is the Quad View setup. This divides the large 3D view into four smaller panes, each displaying a different view of the scene. Usually a perspective view is augmented by three orthogonal (non-perspective) views of the scene.

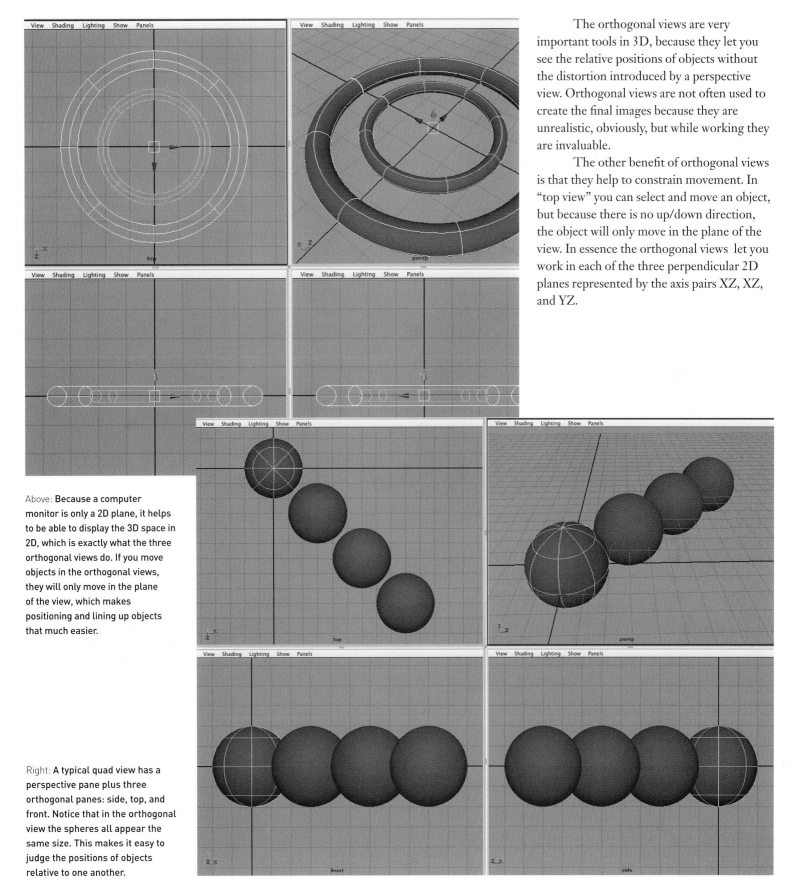

The orthogonal views are very important tools in 3D, because they let you see the relative positions of objects without the distortion introduced by a perspective view. Orthogonal views are not often used to create the final images because they are unrealistic, obviously, but while working they are invaluable.

The other benefit of orthogonal views is that they help to constrain movement. In "top view" you can select and move an object, but because there is no up/down direction, the object will only move in the plane of the view. In essence the orthogonal views let you work in each of the three perpendicular 2D planes represented by the axis pairs XZ, XZ, and YZ.

Above: **Because a computer monitor is only a 2D plane, it helps to be able to display the 3D space in 2D, which is exactly what the three orthogonal views do. If you move objects in the orthogonal views, they will only move in the plane of the view, which makes positioning and lining up objects that much easier.**

Right: **A typical quad view has a perspective pane plus three orthogonal panes: side, top, and front. Notice that in the orthogonal view the spheres all appear the same size. This makes it easy to judge the positions of objects relative to one another.**

GEOMETRY CONCEPTS As we've seen, the coordinate system lets us define points in space, join these points together to form 2D shapes, and link these shapes to make 3D surfaces. When we do this, we are creating 3D models or "geometry," which is what 3D graphics are all about.

Aside from some special circumstances (such as volumetric rendering) you need to have geometry in order to create a 3D image. The process of building geometry is called modeling, and as with coordinates there are some simple rules and concepts at work.

Working backward, we have a full 3D model, which can be lit and rendered to create an image or animation. The model can be thought of as the uppermost geometric level, and within it are sublevels known as components. Below the model we have faces, also known as polygons; below polygons we have edges; and at the base component level, we have points. When we select and move an object, we are really moving all its components at once, maintaining their relative positions. To the computer this is easy, but to us it would be impossible to keep track of all those coordinates.

If we want to change the shape of the model we can edit its components, first by entering a special mode in the 3D program's interface, selecting the desired component level, selecting the desired components, and moving them. Usually we just click a button

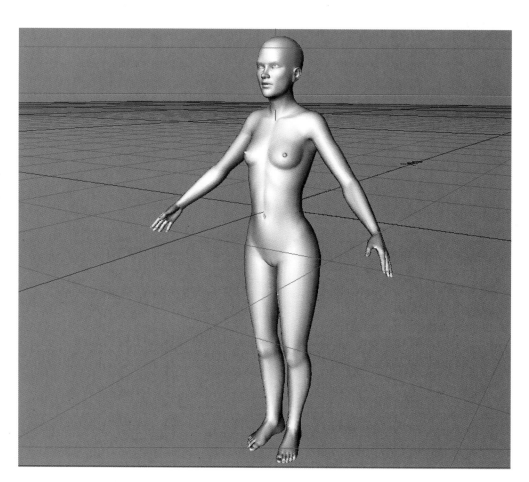

to enter, say, Point Editing mode. The tools usually used to move the entire object now only apply to points that we select. If our object is a character, we could select the points on the end of her nose and move them to make her nose longer.

The geometry described here is polygonal, but as we'll see later there are other types of geometry, each with different components with different properties.

Above: **3D geometry has several levels. First there is the object as a whole. This is the model that is animated and rendered. We can move it as if it were a single solid object.**

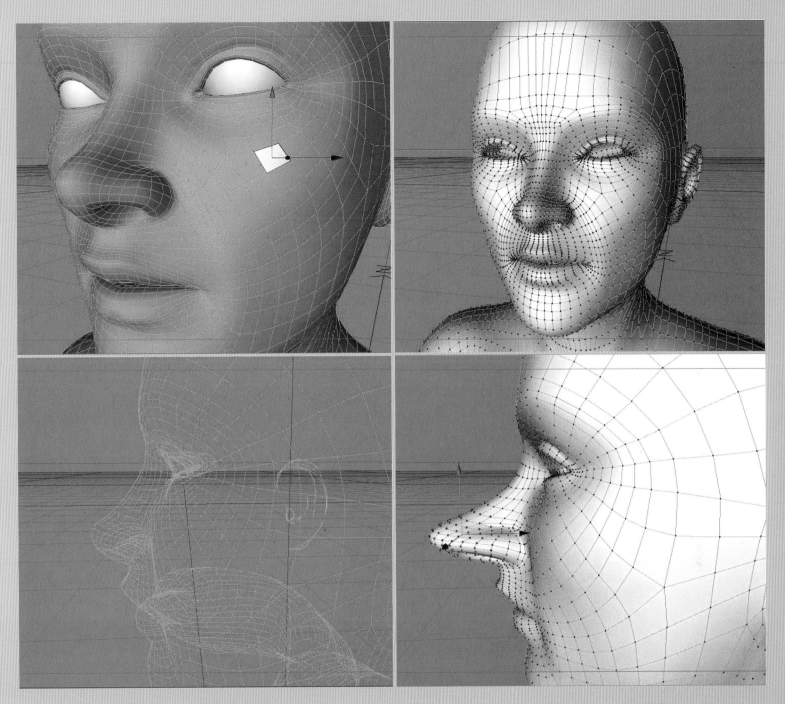

Top left: The solid object is made from a net of connected faces called polygons. Each polygon is a flat face, joined to its neighbor through sharing points and edges.

Above: The next component level is the edge. Edges mark the boundaries of polygons and enclose them.

Top right: At the lowest component level is the point. Points are connected to make edges, and each edge connects only two points.

Above: By entering component-editing mode, we can select the desired components of a mode and move, scale, rotate, or stretch them to change its shape, here making a character's nose longer.

SHADING AND DISPLAY RENDERING In and of themselves, points and edges in 3D are invisible: they define positions inside the computer, but they have no physical property. You can make them visible, however, by drawing a dot or line to represent them on the computer. A model can therefore be represented as a "wireframe" by drawing its edges.

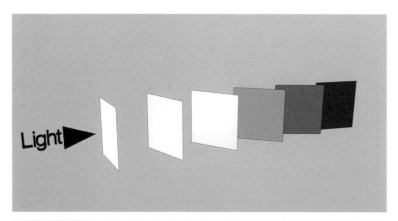

Wireframe models are useful during construction because they let you see the structure of the surface and the components. They are not so good for final rendering—unless you want to convey a deliberate digital or CG style. The good thing about them is that they are easy for the computer to calculate, and therefore quick to display. A model can easily be rotated in real time inside a 3D program using the wireframe display mode.

When it comes to final rendering we don't want to see the components—we just want to see a smooth surface that looks solid and real. For this we need shading. Shading is the process of filling in a model's polygons, taking into

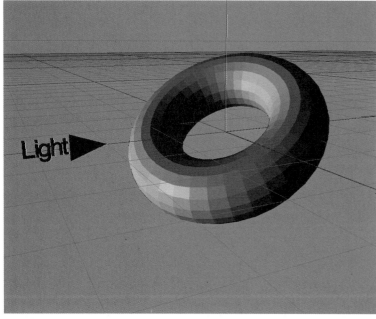

Top: **Flat shading takes the angle between the polygon and the light in the scene into account and fills in the polygon with a flat color. The shallower the angle, the darker the polygon.**

Above: **The problem with flat shading is that you end up seeing each polygon, giving a faceted appearance to objects.**

Above: **By interpolating the angles between polygons, each pixel in the render is varied in shade. This creates the appearance of a smooth surface.**

part 04. 3D core concepts

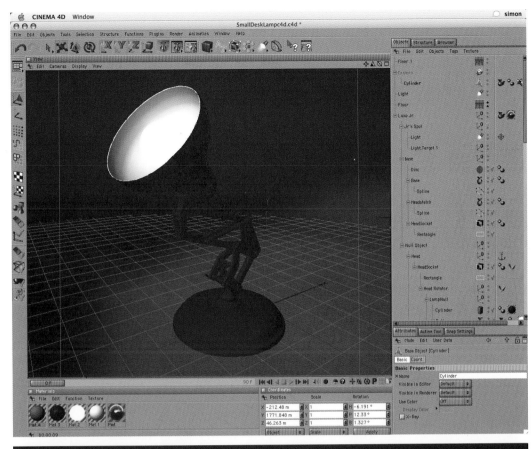

Above left: Here's a scene displayed in OpenGL in the 3D program's interface. The aim is to provide good visual feedback of surface shading, textures, and lighting while also offering very fast scene interaction. Absolute image quality is not as important.

Below left: The same scene rendered with the software's final-quality renderer is not accelerated by OpenGL graphics cards so it's slower but offers much higher quality. Notice the shadows, reflections, and smoother edges.

consideration the direction of light in a scene. One way to do that is to assign a single color to each polygon depending on its angle to the light rays. Polygons facing head-on are shaded at full brightness; those tilted away are darker until they are full edge on or facing in the opposite direction to the light, when they will be shaded black.

Smooth shading uses a more complex algorithm that interpolates the shading between polygons, varying and blending the shading to eliminate the hard breaks in the illumination and to make objects appear smoother. Two common types of smooth shading are Phong and Blinn: you'll often come across these terms in 3D graphics.

Using the power of graphics cards and a special API called OpenGL, a branch of rendering called display rendering has developed, specifically designed with the 3D artist in mind (though it has other uses, too, such as games and medical visualization). Its aim is to accelerate the display of shaded models as they are moved in real-time on the computer screen. While it's different to the software-rendered final image that is output to disk as a still image or animation, it gives a more accurate idea than smooth shading.

FINAL RENDERING Final rendering is the process of creating the finished artwork or animation, a process that requires two things: a lot of time and a lot of CPU horsepower. That's because rendering involves many, often very complex, calculations that the computer has to work out to create the final image.

Left: If antialiasing is not performed, the image will render much more quickly but areas of high contrast will suffer jagged artifacts called aliasing. Note that, in the zoomed portion, the edges are hard and jagged.

Right: With antialiasing enabled the jagged edges are smoothed out but the render will take longer. Quality always comes at a price.

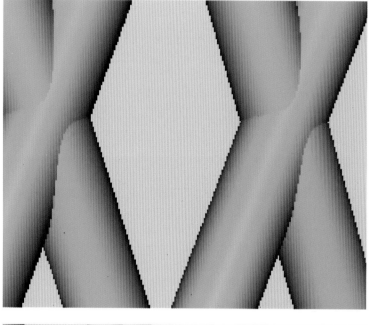

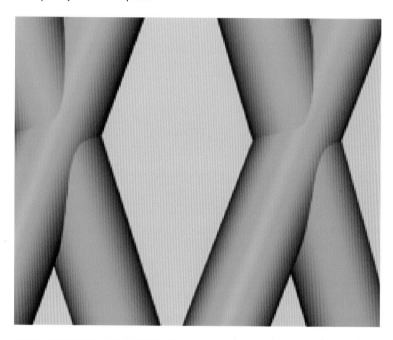

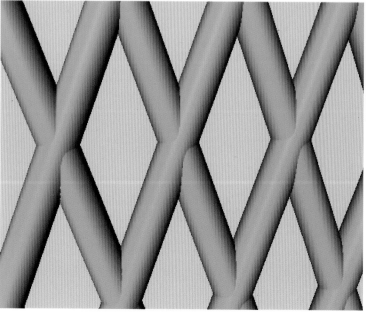

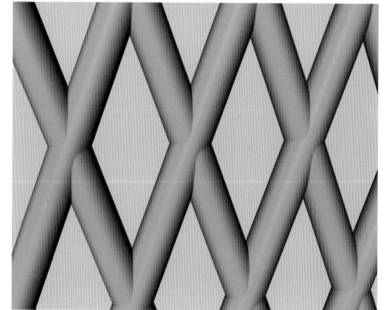

part 04. 3D core concepts

Rendering is always a tricky balancing act between quality and speed. Reflections and refraction, for example, can take so long to render that a 3D artist—or a software designer for that matter—will attempt to minimize these effects or even fake them. Other CPU-intense calculations include advanced lighting effects, such as radiosity rendering, and volumetrics. We'll look at these in more detail later in the book, but for now let's examine the basics.

One reason for creating the final render is to smooth out jagged lines in the image. This process, known as antialiasing, involves sophisticated processes that the CPU and software perform in order to maximize image quality and minimize rendering time.

The simplest way to antialias an image is to render it at twice the size needed, then scale the image down to the desired size. The resampling done to scale the image will average the pixels and smooth them out. On the downside, doubling the image size results in four times as many pixels and four times the render time, which is obviously undesirable.

Adaptive antialiasing analyzes the image during rendering and only antialiases pixels that need it. This is usually done by setting a contrast threshold above which pixels will be antialiased, preventing large flat or low-contrast areas in the image from being unnecessarily antialiased and resulting in greatly reduced rendering times.

Shading is one way to render a scene, but the relatively simple algorithms involved can't calculate the complex effects of reflection or refraction. For this a technique called raytracing was developed. Raytracing casts virtual rays of light into a scene backward, from the camera onto the objects and back toward the light source. This makes sure that only rays of light that end up contributing to the image are calculated. Where a ray strikes an object in the scene, the software looks to see if that pixel is in direct view of a light, then calculates the angle and hence the color of the pixel. If the object is reflective, the ray shoots off farther into the scene. If it strikes another object, that object will appear as a reflection in the first object's surface. It sounds complex—and it is—which is why raytracing takes longer than Phong shading.

Most 3D programs use adaptive or hybrid rendering to get the best of both worlds. When an object is reflective, or transparent and refractive, raytracing is use. If no raytracing is needed, those objects are simply shaded. Using adaptive raytracing, you get the best of both worlds. Objects that are not reflective or refractive are scanline-rendered, while raytracing is used only for the areas that need it.

Below: **Shaded rendering, also known as scanline rendering, does not take into account things like reflections and refraction. As a result it's quick to render. The time taken is 58 seconds.**

Bottom: **Raytracing uses virtual light rays cast into the scene to calculate complex effects like reflections and refraction. Here's the same scene rendered with raytracing. The time taken is 4 minutes and 34 seconds.**

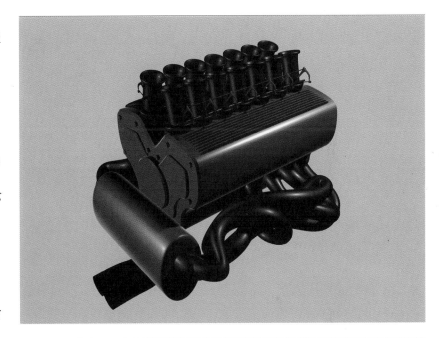

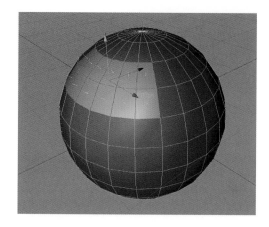

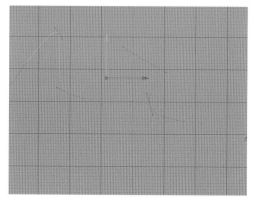

PART 04. 3D CORE CONCEPTS

CHAPTER TWO

MODELING

Modeling is the first step in producing a 3D image or animation. Except for a few special cases, you can't render anything if you don't have some objects to render. In other words, you need to get building before you can do anything else. Modeling—like rendering—requires a balance of quality and speed, which makes it important to bear certain pointers in mind as you make your 3D model.

There are two aspects of the speed equation. First, the more complex a model is, the longer it will take to build. Second, the more polygons an object has, the longer it will take to render. Actually 3D programs can handle very large data sets quite efficiently, so the rendering consideration is not quite as important as, for example, knowing how many objects will need raytracing. The problems come when you are creating a dense and visually rich scene, such as a model of a city, thick undergrowth, or a fleet of space ships. It will take a long time to render, but the pressing concern is that the amount of geometry used can slow the display rendering

system down to a crawl, which makes it difficult to work with. In the worst cases, very large scenes can even cause some systems to run out of memory and applications to grind to a halt!

The weight of a polygon model—or how many polygons make it up—is also important if the model is going to be used in a real-time applications, such as a simulation or a computer game. A games console costing $200 won't have the 3D power of your graphics workstation, meaning that a special branch of modeling—low-polygon modeling—is dedicated to this concern.

Either way, the golden rule of modeling is, "If you won't see it, don't build it." This rule applies, without exception, to every single modeling situation. Make it your daily mantra until you know instinctively what and what not to model before you start. Of course planning will help, especially for animations. If you work out a shot beforehand you'll know which parts of the objects in the scene will need the most detail and which can be more roughly modeled.

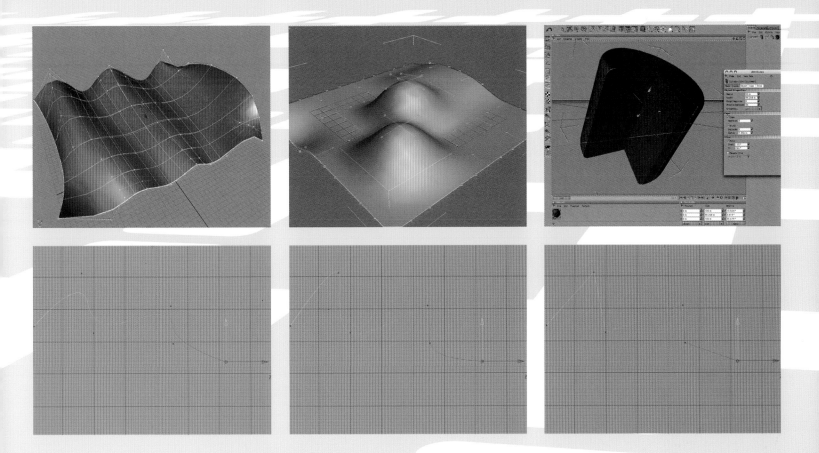

Top row, left to right: **Polygons are the simplest kind of geometry in 3D. With polygons what you see is what you get, but they can be unwieldy—especially if you need to edit an object containing hundreds or thousands of them.**

NURBS, unlike polygons, are resolution-independent. You can set how fine the surface is displayed without rebuilding the object. NURBS surfaces are controlled by fewer points, called control points, than polygons so it's easier to create and edit smoothly flowing shapes with NURBS than polygons.

Patches, or Bezier surfaces as they are sometimes known, are similar to NURBS surfaces but are created using a different underlying technology. Bezier patches often have handles on their points that allow you to modify the curvature of the surface.

Parametric objects are like small programs in themselves that generate a particular 3D form. You will often have access to the parameters that define their shape, hence their name.

Bottom row, left to right: **Curves are special kinds of objects in 3D. They are not renderable in themselves but are used during construction of 3D surfaces. A curve may be created using a variety of different algorithms to define how the curve** is interpolated through its control points. Those familiar with illustration packages will be used to Bezier curves, though there are also NURBS, linear and cubic types, as well as others, depending on the 3D program.

Polygons are not the only kind of geometry used in modeling. Curves, NURBS, and patches offer an alternative approach. NURBS are resolution-independent surfaces that define smooth curves using many fewer points than a polygon model. While a polygon circle might need 100 or more points to look smooth, a NURBS circle needs only four (see p80 for more on NURBS). Bezier patches are similar to NURBS, but the points have handles, like the curves in a 2D drawing program. You simply draw a line between two points, then use one or more handles to drag it out into other, smoothly curved shapes. In fact, curves appear in 3D modeling, operating as 2D versions of NURBS and bezier patch surfaces.

Other kinds of geometry include parametric and analytic primitives: ready-made, simple, solid forms, such as spheres, cones, tori, planes, or cylinders, generated on the fly. They have no editable components as such, but you may have access to the parameters that define them, such as a sphere's radius or a cone's height.

BASIC POLYGONAL MODELING

In the early days of 3D graphics you had to create objects point by point, or write a script or program to generate forms based on mathematical formulas. That's fine for research, or for visualizing math functions and topologies, but as far as we know there is no function to generate a dinosaur, watch, or motorcycle, or many of the other innumerable objects in everyday life.

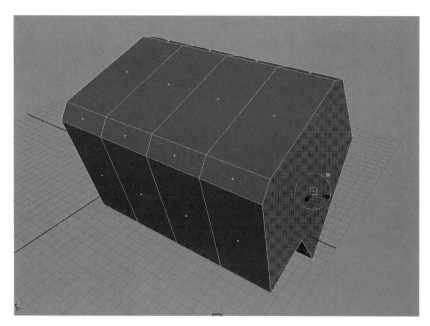

What we need is a tool set—one that takes the drudgery out of modeling point by point but enables us to create any kind of object we can imagine. 3D programs do this by offering simple procedure-based tools or commands. When it comes to polygon modeling, there are four very simple tools that take a flat 2D polygon or a curve and turn it into a 3D surface: Extrude, Lathe, Sweep, and Loft.

In order to create a 3D polygonal surface, you can begin with a 2D polygon shape or curve, then run one of the four commands on it. Here are the results using a polygon and a curve.

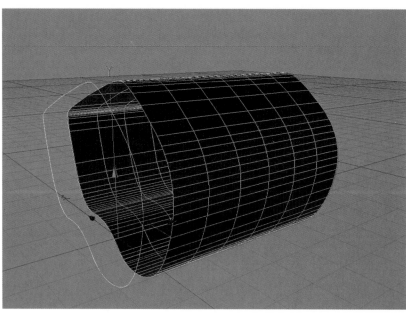

Left above: **Extruding simply moves the polygon along a certain direction, creating a surface whose cross-section is the polygon shape. You'll often have the option to specify how many subdivisions you require—or how smooth the polygon mesh will be—along the extrusion direction. Note that the surface has the same resolution as the initial polygon.**

Left: **When you extrude a curve the same thing happens, except the curve is tessellated into polygons during extrusion. You will usually be able to specify the accuracy of the tessellation; the closer the match between the curve and the polygon surface, the greater the number of polygons required. The tessellation is usually adaptive, so that more polygons are used only where needed.**

Below, left and right: Lathing the polygon or curve rotates it around a chosen axis, or sometimes around another curve. The resulting object is rotationally symmetrical, so it's an obvious choice to create vases, bottles, plates, and other rotationally symmetrical objects.

Bottom left: Sweeping is similar to extruding, except the direction of extrusion is governed by another polygon or curve. Sometimes you have the option to scale or rotate the profile as it is swept, to create a tapering or twisting surface.

Bottom right: Lofting (also known as loafing or skinning) requires multiple source profiles in order to work, taking several cross-sections and stringing a surface across them—like the cross-members in a boat hull. If these are all the same then the result is much the same as extruding or sweeping, or even lathing (there's usually more than one way to get the same result in 3D). However, if the profiles are different, lofting lets you create surfaces that would be impossible using the other three methods.

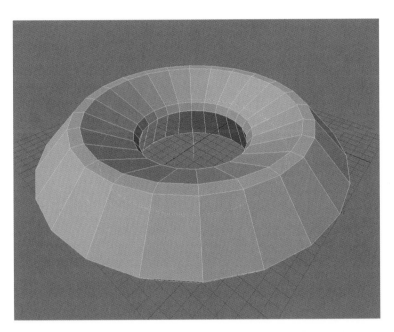

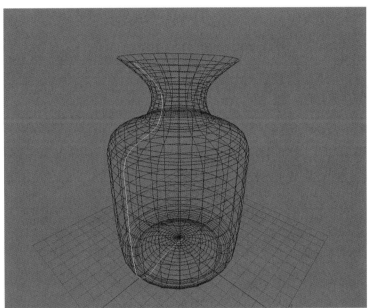

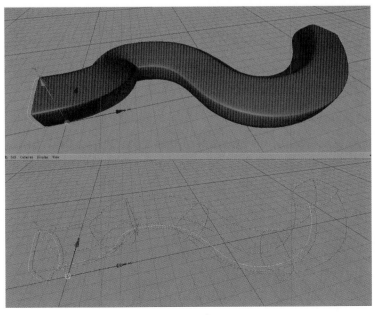

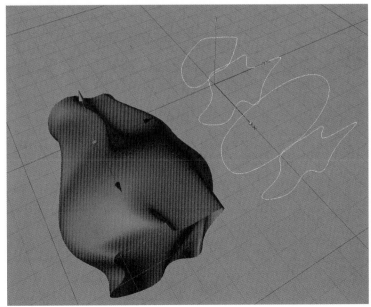

NURBS MODELING

NURBS MODELING With polygon modeling the polygons can be connected together in any way you like to create a surface. A polygon may have three, four, or many points and a polygon object can consist of any combination of polygons. Polygons are said to have arbitrary topology (topology is the structure of a surface), but NURBS are totally different.

With NURBS you can only create a surface one way—with a grid of NURBS curves. It's like making a shape out of wire netting: you can mold and bend it but the wires always cross each other in a gridlike pattern.

One set of points forms a row called the U direction, and another set of points at 90° forms the V direction. To visualize it, imagine you draw a NURBS circle. That circle represents U. Extrude the circle to form a cylinder, and you get the V direction. The U direction goes around the cylinder, the V direction along it. Even if you bend the cylinder, you still have points in U and V: their relationship doesn't change, only the shape of the surface in 3D space.

The implications of this very rigid topology means that you can't extend NURBS surfaces in the same way as polygonal ones (see p84 on polygon detailing). But you can do some other nifty things because, unlike polygon objects, the computer "knows" a lot about the nature of the surface topology. For example, you can add extra geometry wherever you need it. If you want an extra row of points in U or V (or both) then it's a simple matter to add one anywhere along the object's surface.

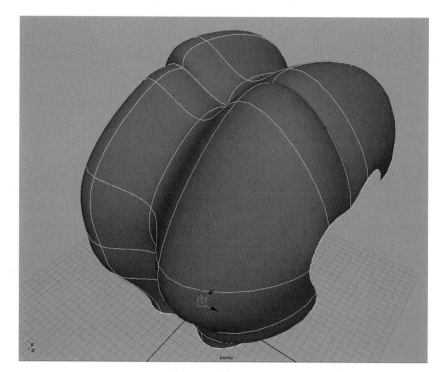

Another cool thing with NURBS is that you can get the 3D program to blend between two surfaces, adding a new surface in between and getting both ends to match precisely the ends of the existing surfaces. You can also project curves onto surfaces to deform them and to build off surfaces accurately. However because the topology of NURBS surfaces is so rigid, you can't cut holes in them.

There is a workaround called trimming. Trimming uses projected curves to define a hole or a slice on a NURBS surface. The NURBS surface isn't itself cut, but during rendering, which requires the surface to be tessellated (converted into polygons), the hole can be created simply by leaving out those polygons inside the trim curve.

It's important to note that most 3D programs cannot render or shade NURBS surfaces directly. In order to do this they have to be tessellated. The conversion is only done for display and rendering purposes, and the fineness of the tessellation can be set depending on your requirements, making NURBS objects resolution-independent.

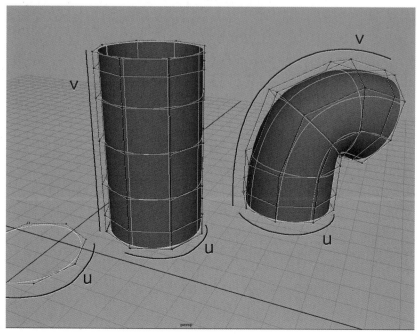

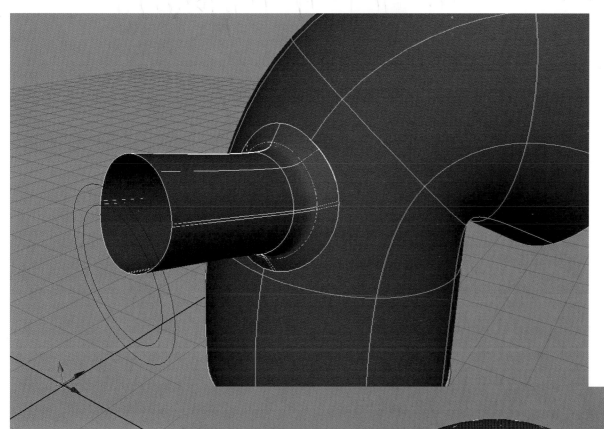

Left: **NURBS** curves can be projected onto NURBS surfaces and subsequently used for further modeling. Here two circles are projected and used to create a smoothly blended fillet joining the two surfaces.

Below: **Trimming can make holes and slice NURBS surfaces. This is an illusion because only the tessellated representation of the NURBS surface has the hole.**

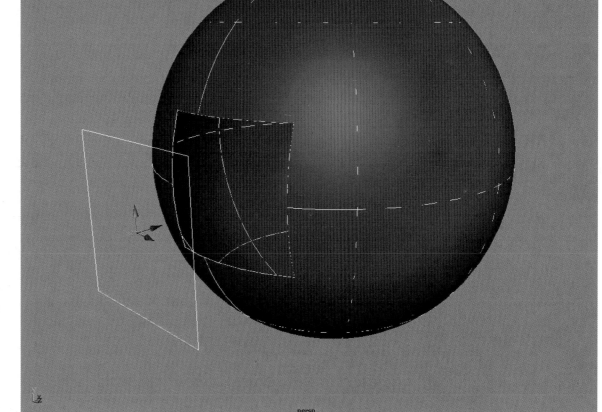

Opposite above: A **NURBS** surface, no matter what its shape, always has two well-defined directions called U and V: the surface is defined by a net of control points arranged in a gridlike pattern. Isoparms on the surface (the green lines) display the direction of this grid.

Opposite below: A **NURBS** circle is a string of points in the U direction (curves are always designated as being the U direction), but extrude the circle and you add the V direction. Even if you bend the resulting surface you still have U and V directions on the surface.

SUBDIVISION SURFACES

We've seen two very different modeling technologies in NURBS and polygons. Both have their strengths and weaknesses, and you may find one better suited to certain tasks than others. Wouldn't it be great if there were a modeling technology that combined the resolution independence of NURBS and the arbitrary topology of polygons? Well there is, and it's called subdivision surface modeling, or SubDs for short.

With SubDs, you take a polygonal object and attach a subdivision algorithm to it. This is not like the usual polygonal subdivide commands. Not only is it continuously calculated, but it also smoothes out the shape, making it more rounded and organic-looking. It also tends to shrink the object's volume, and as a result you get an effect on-screen that looks a lot like a NURBS object: a coarse outer cage of control points that subtend a higher resolution, smoothed surface beneath it. The outer cage behaves just like any other polygon object, so all your polygon modeling skills and tools can be used on it, except you only need a fraction of the polygons in the

Below left: **Here is an organic object made with ordinary polygons. Notice how many polygons are needed to create the illusion or a continuous, smooth surface. Making changes is difficult because it is so easy to disrupt the continuity of the surface.**

Below right: **The same object made with subdivision surface is an order of magnitude easier to build and edit. Note that the rounded edges on the smoothed surface get tighter the closer together the points are on the cage. This makes it easy to create nice rounded edges of any radius on your objects.**

cage to create a very high resolution, smooth surface. This makes editing extremely easy since there are far fewer points, polygons, and edges to deal with.

Subdivision surfaces are resolution-independent. This means that you can set the resolution (the number of subdivisions used to smooth the surface) of the resulting surface independently of the cage. Often you will also have the option of setting different resolutions for display and final rendering. This means you can model efficiently in your 3D program without the display getting bogged down by thousands of polygons, but when you render you'll see a perfectly smooth object.

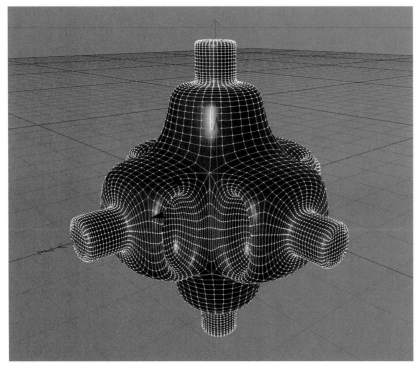
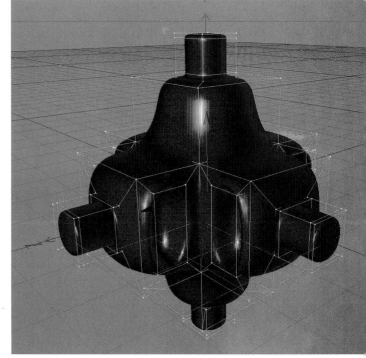

Left: You can change the resolution of a SubD surface whenever you like. From left to right are three different subdivision levels, 0, 1, and 2. The surface appears smoother with increasing subdivision levels. Note that a level of 0 denotes no smoothing, so you see the cage object as it is.

Below: When the scene is rendered, all three look identical because they all have their rendering subdivision set to 3.

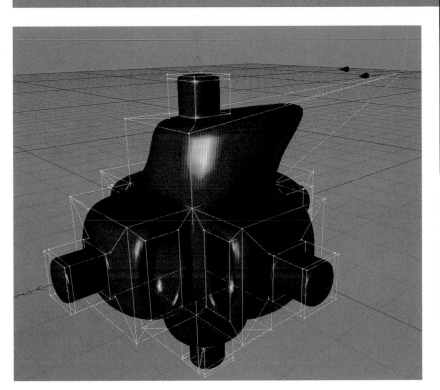

Left: Moving a single point on the SubD object cage causes the underlying surface to move along with it smoothly and with continuity. Note that the caged object is usually displayed in wireframe mode so that you can see the surface beneath. Often this is done automatically by the software.

POLYGON DETAILING If you want to add details to polygon objects that have already been created, you need a finer toolset. By selecting certain polygons on an existing 3D object, you can extend the object or add local detail to it. For example, you might add a handle to a mug or the holes to a telephone dial.

The Extrude tool can be useful here, but the other three—Sweep, Lathe, and Loft—are not usually as practical. Luckily, some other common tools come into play at this point. These detailing tools are used to modify 3D objects and, in any 3D program worth its salt, all of these tools will be interactive. Clicking and dragging with the mouse activates the tool and varies the degree of effect, which should make polygon modeling feel quite intuitive and hands-on. Note that these tools work with both polygon and subdivision surface modeling.

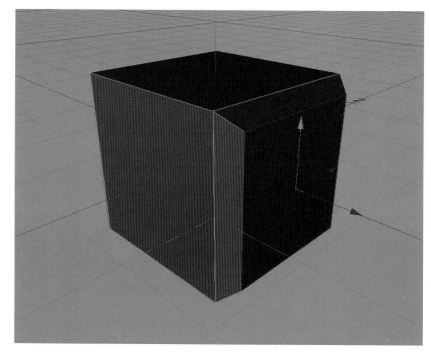

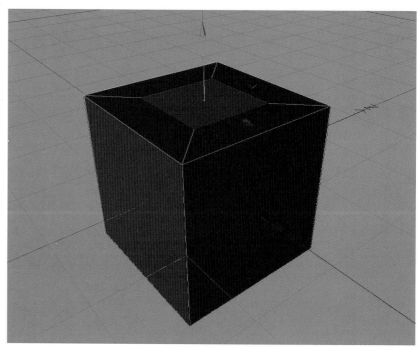

Above right: **Beveling is similar to** extruding, except the shifted polygon is scaled inward or outward, creating a chamfered or beveled edge. Depending on the program, Beveling can be applied to points, edges, and faces, with different results for each.

Below right: **Inner Bevel (or Inset)** is like a Bevel but with no offset. A second polygon is created matching the first inside it and connected at each corner. It only applies to faces.

Below: Knifing lets you slice in extra edges on an object as if you cut it with a knife. The extra geometry can then be edited and the object remains in one piece; it isn't cut in two. Knifing is useful if you realized that you have insufficient points and edges to make the model work. In this example a capsule is knifed twice then the resulting section extruded inward to create a recessed swathe.

Bottom: Welding takes two or more points and merges them into one. This is a way to reduce the amount of geometry or join two separate polygon sections together. In this example, the two points on the right are selected, then welded to give the result on the left.

Below: A Split or Cut tool is similar to a Knife tool but only some 3D programs have it. Unlike knifing, which cuts all the way through a model, a Split tool works on the surface, slicing only the polygons you want cut and adding geometry in a more controlled way.

Bottom: Subdivide does what it says. It will subdivide selected polygons to add extra geometry. Subdividing is not quite as useful as it sounds though because it rarely gives you enough control over the effect. If you need to use it, it usually means there's a problem with the resolution or that you haven't planned your model properly.

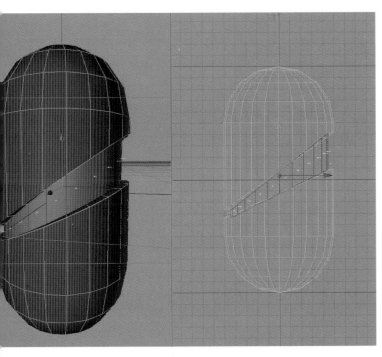

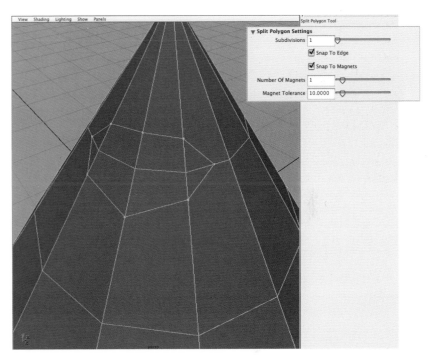

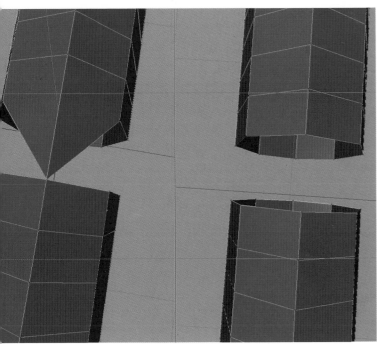

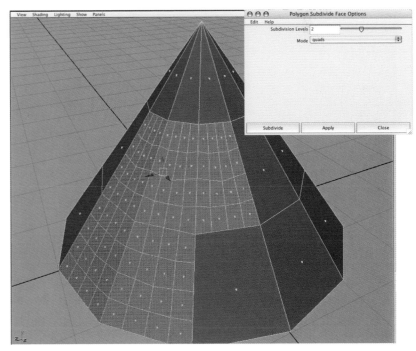

TESSELLATION AND RESOLUTION One of the most common problems you'll come across in 3D is poor-quality models. Apart from bad artistic design, poorly planned models often suffer incorrect tessellation or the wrong resolution. Too high a resolution means that the model will be overly heavy requiring a lot more RAM to render and slowing the interactive OpenGL display, making it difficult to work with. Too low a resolution will make an object that's supposed to be smooth and continuous appear choppy and faceted.

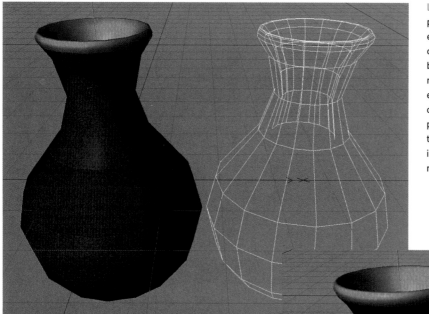

Left: A model with too few polygons looks choppy and coarse, especially at the edges. Circular objects are typical candidates, because you need sufficient numbers of polygons to make the edge of the circle smooth and continuous. If there aren't enough polygons, the edge looks choppy. If the model is to be viewed close-up in a photoreal render, this would not be acceptable.

Below: You get a smoother and more realistic object if you increase the number of polygons used to define it. This vase was created by lathing a curve. We can increase the number of polygons generated by the lathe operation in the lathe parameters. In some programs you will have to do this before you create the lathe, while in others that have a modeling history feature, you can change the resolution whenever you like.

When we talk about the resolution of an object it is usually irrespective of whether the geometry used to construct it is polygonal, NURBS, or something else. This is because at render-time, all types of geometry have to be converted into polygons so that they can be raytraced or shaded by the 3D program's render engine. This process, called tessellation, involves converting a surface into triangles. Triangles cannot be bent so will always render correctly, which is why they are used. There are a few exceptions to this rule, in that a handful of 3D programs are able to render NURBS or patches directly. Most don't, which means it's vital to understand the tessellation process so that you always have the right resolution for your models.

part 04. 3D core concepts

Right: **NURBS** describe curved surfaces with mathematical perfection. However, in order to see them rendered you have to convert this perfect ideal surface into cumbersome polygons at render-time. This is done by the renderer, based on a setting for the accuracy of the conversion. The higher the accuracy, the better the surface will look when rendered.

Below: **Low resolution is desirable** in some circumstances, notably in any real-time applications such as computer games or for Web 3D. The low resolution of the objects can be compensated for by clever use of modeling and texture maps.

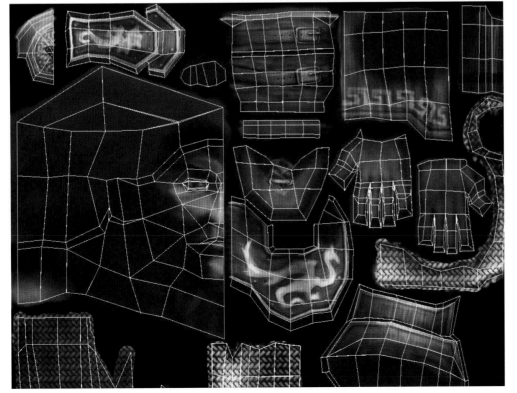

When modeling, it's important to think ahead and plan which objects need to have a high resolution and which don't. Generally the rule is: the closer the object is to the camera, the higher its resolution needs to be. Note that objects that do not have curves or rounded edges will not need a high resolution; flat sides can be represented easily with single polygons. You only need to worry about curves and organic shapes.

NURBS surfaces also need to have their resolution defined. Internally, the NURBS surface describes curved surfaces perfectly; what you are doing when you set the tessellation level is to define how accurate the approximation of the surface will be when it is tessellated in polygon form for rendering.

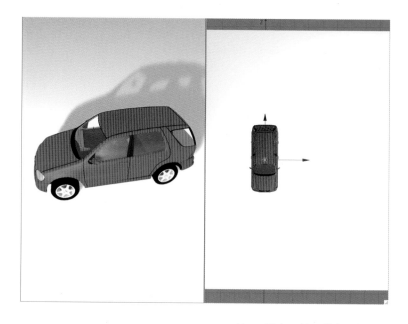

Above: **High ambient light values can wash out a scene, making it look flat and lifeless. It can be useful for special effects, though, such as creating deliberately flat and cartoonlike images.**

PART 04. 3D CORE CONCEPTS

CHAPTER THREE

LIGHT AND SURFACE

In the 3D scene—as in reality—nothing is visible without light, or rather, lights. In 3D applications these are objects in the scene, placed to illuminate the scene in much the same way as lighting on a film set or in a photographic studio does. There are four main kinds of lights in 3D: point, spot, distant, and area. They each have different properties and are used to simulate certain characteristics of real light and to get specific looks.

The point light, also known as an omni, is the simplest kind of light. It mimics a point light source, such as a bulb, by shining radially in all directions. The position of a point light relative to other objects is important because it will greatly affect the scene's illumination. Conversely, rotating a point light makes no difference at all because its illumination is symmetrical.

A distant light is the opposite of a point light. A distant light, also known as a parallel light or infinite light, mimics the effect of the sun or any very distant light source. It does this by shining parallel light rays into the scene. Despite the fact that a parallel light will often

exist as an object in the scene with a position, moving it has no effect on the illumination it provides. Rotating a distant light will change its illumination, however, because you are changing the direction of the parallel light rays it casts.

A spotlight is similar to a point light except that it casts its rays in a cone shape rather than spherically. Spotlights are easy to get to grips with because they closely mimic their real-world counterparts. The illumination they cast changes if they are moved or rotated, so in this respect they are very controllable, letting you put light exactly where you want it—not where you don't. Spotlights have adjustable cone angles, giving them a range of focus or "spread" from very wide to very tight. They usually have either separate inner and outer cone angles, or a single "soft edge" parameter to make the edge of the cone very hard, very soft, or anything in between.

Area lights are a special case. These cast light from an extended area rather than a single point, much like a photographer's light diffuser (a square box with an open end or frame covered with a diffusing material behind which a light is placed) or a window in daylight. Like spotlights their rotation affects their illumination, but not by the same degree.

Ambient light is a special class of illumination. Adding ambient light in a 3D program is akin to setting the brightness of the darkest areas in the scene greater than 0. It pervades the whole scene, with the result that too much will wash the scene out and reduce overall contrast. Ambient light should, therefore, only be used sparingly if photorealism is your ultimate goal. Notice that each light's shadow is markedly different.

Below left: **Point lights are like naked lightbulbs, casting illumination in all directions into the scene from a single point.**

Bottom left: **Parallel lights mimic a very distant light source, like the Sun. The light rays are parallel and do not start at a particular location but extend infinitely. Despite the scene object having a position, moving a distant light does not change the illumination of the scene, but rotating it does.**

Below: **A spotlight casts its light in a cone. You can vary the cone angle to make very light, focused lights or broad ones.**

Bottom right: **Area lights have a more subtle effect on a scene. Their light is spread over an area, making them good for creating large panels of light such as from an open window.**

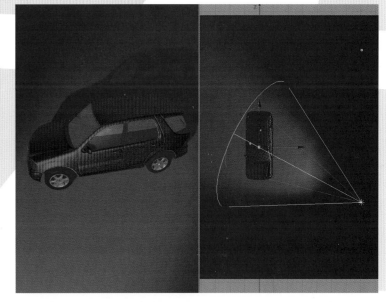

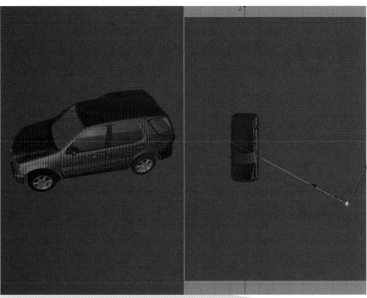

CAMERAS The virtual camera is a very important concept in 3D. Not only does a camera provide a point of view from which to view your 3D scene, it offers a great deal of control over the look and feel of a 3D image. 3D cameras are designed to mimic real cameras, so you'll often find exactly the same kinds of controls on the virtual cameras as on a real camera, such as field of view, lens type, or zoom.

The camera exists as a scene object that can be moved and rotated and, of course, animated. Positioning the camera is crucial for achieving the desired look and feel for your render and great care should be taken when devising the composition of a scene.

Usually there are two cameras at work in a 3D scene. You won't often realize the first one is a camera—it's the perspective view of the scene displayed in the main 3D view. Although there might not be an associated scene object, the display shown in a perspective view is generated in exactly the same way as if you viewed the scene through a virtual camera. And there is more you can do when the camera is an object in the scene, including all sorts of clever animation tricks, such as linking it to an animated object so that it moves along to track it.

A narrow camera angle and very distant camera creates a foreshortening effect on objects. Perspective distortion is reduced and objects can appear a bit flat.

When using a virtual camera, the two controls that have the greatest effect over the appearance of the scene are the zoom value and position. When you zoom a camera you increase its field of view. If you imagine the camera's view as a pyramid extending from its apex out into the scene, the width of the pyramid is the camera's field of view (or viewing angle). Zoom into a scene, and the camera stays put but its viewing angle decreases. Zoom out and the viewing angle increases. As in real-world photography, wide-angle views cause visible distortion of objects, which can be used to dramatic effect when composing your scene.

Strangely enough, virtual cameras don't actually share the visual artifacts present in real cameras—they're optically perfect. However, because we expect to see these "defects" in real images, computer graphics programs have to put these artifacts back, often at great expense in rendering time.

One typical artifact is depth of field, or DOF for short. DOF causes some objects to be in focus and others to be out of focus. Re-creating this in a 3D camera requires some trickery on the part of the 3D program, but the results are often much more realistic and organic looking. Other artifacts that can be simulated include barrel distortion, chromatic aberration, and motion blur. The latter is essential for animation, because without it fast-moving objects look totally fake.

part 04. 3D core concepts

Above: **Using a wide camera angle with the camera close to an object results in exaggerated perspective, which is quite dramatic. The distortion helps to communicate the form of the object and gives an image more depth.**

Right: **Motion blurring and depth of field are two crucial characteristics of real camera images that have to be simulated in 3D. Motion blurring especially is essential for realistic CG animation.**

ANIMATION is the process of changing a value over time, either position, rotation, scale, or some other value, such as the intensity of a light or the color of a material. Animation in a 3D program is achieved using a process called keyframing. The term harks back to traditional 2D cel animation. A lead animator would block out the key poses of a character while junior animators would draw the frames in between to create the fully animated sequence.

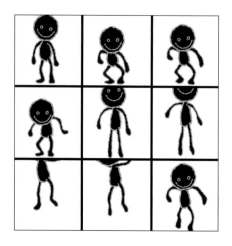

Left: In 2D animation, keyframes, drawn by a lead animator, show the character's main poses in a sequence. The keyframes are joined together by junior animators who create the in-between frames.

Below: An animated object's keyframes can also be viewed in a timeline. This is a simplified display of the keyframes, showing each as a marker on a line. The positions of the keyframes can be moved to alter the timing of the animation.

on the horizontal. By default, 3D programs will interpolate linearly between keyframe values; the function curve is a straight diagonal line. However in the function curve we can also change the interpolation to create different kinds of motion. A typical way to do this is to make the curve an S shape. When you do this you change the acceleration, i.e., the rate of change of the value. An S-shaped curve will cause the value to change slowly at first, then accelerate to maximum rate of change, then smoothly decelerate to a stop. This is very useful for position and rotation animation since real objects need time to reach their full speed or come to a stop. This kind of S-shape curve is often referred to as ease-in/ease-out animation.

The principle of keyframes is exactly the same in a 3D program, except instead of a hoard of animators doing the leg work, the computer does it all for you.

To animate the position of an object in 3D, you record a keyframe, move to a different time in the sequence, move the object, and record another keyframe. The computer smoothly interpolates between the values in the two keyframes to create the animation, which can then be played back in real time or rendered.

Whatever the parameter being animated, it's important to remember that it is just a number changing over time. Because of this you can get a better idea of how the value is being interpolated over time using a graph called a function curve. Function curves display the animated data as a curve, with the value on the vertical axis and time

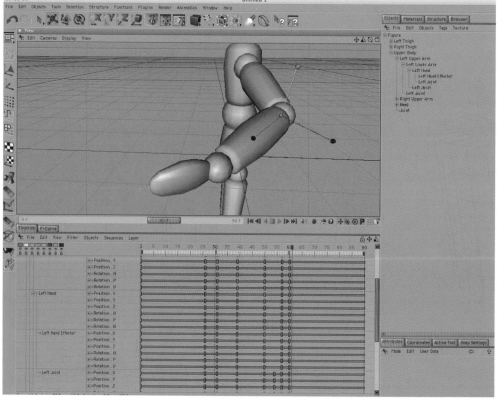

part 04. 3D core concepts

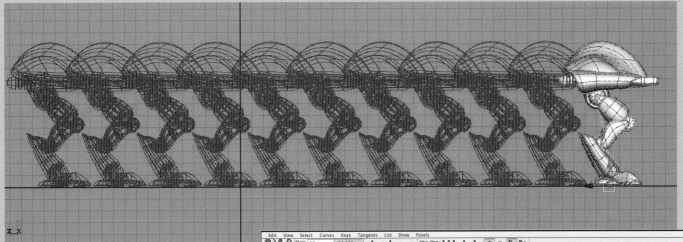

Above and right: **A function curve displays the rate of change of a keyframed value over time as a curve on a graph. Here is the default linear interpolation curve for an object's position. The object would start instantaneously reaching full speed, and stop equally abruptly. The purple wireframes show the position of the object at each frame of the animation: note their regular spacing.**

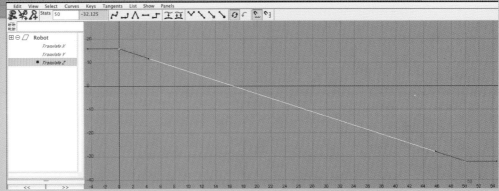

Above and right: **A more natural ease-in/ease-out interpolation can be created by changing the shape of the curve by using its Bezier handles in an S-shape. The object will now accelerate and decelerate smoothly.**

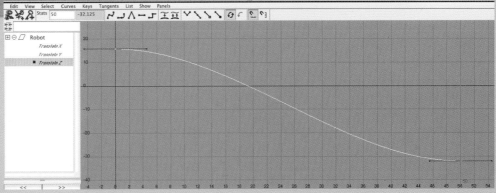

MATERIALS AND TEXTURES Modeling can only achieve so much when it comes to the details. While there is a simple beauty in a plain, well-built 3D model, materials and textures applied to the model's surface make 3D objects appear truly lifelike.

Take note: the actual terms used can vary from program to program. For our purposes, we'll use the convention that the word "material" refers to a group of properties that define the overall look of an object's surface, while a "texture" is a bitmap image applied to an object in one of the Material channels.

A material is a set of properties used by the rendering engine to shade an object's surface. There are many different implementations of material systems, but usually a material consists of a set of channels such as Color, Luminance, Reflection, Transparency, Specular, and Bump. Together, these define the surface's basic qualities. With this simple set of controls you can simulate a wide variety of substances from glass to metal and plastic, fabric, and even organic matter, such as skin and foliage.

Although you can set a color or value for some of the parameters in a material, you can also use a bitmap image as a texture map, and this is where the real fun begins. In some channels, such as Bump, it only makes sense to use a bitmap image, and bumps are a good place to start when it comes to explaining texture maps.

A bump texture map is simply a grayscale image applied to the Bump channel of a material. When the material is applied to an object and rendered, areas that are white in the bump map are rendered as surface protrusions, and areas that are black as depressions. All shades in between represent a variety of bump depths, with 50% gray being perfectly flat.

Color textures can also be applied to materials in the Color channel and together with bump maps can be used to simulate a huge amount of fine surface detail not present in the model's geometry. Knowing what details to model and what to leave for texturing is the key to achieving really high quality, realistic renders.

Above: The fine details of the skin in this render are created using very large, high resolution textures. Modeling such fine details would be extremely time-consuming—this is the real power of texturing in 3D.

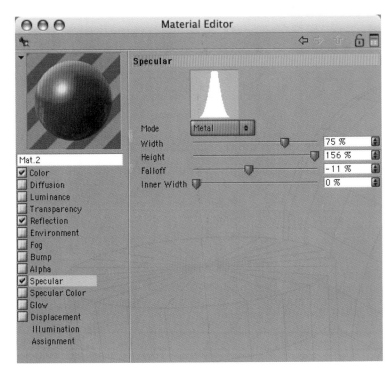

Above: A typical material system looks like this. Down the left side you can see a list of the available channels and in the right are displayed the parameters for the currently selected channel, Specular in this case. There's also a preview ball, which gives you an idea of what the material will look like when rendered.

Below: A selection of materials is displayed, each of which uses exactly the same set of material channels, just with different values in each.

Below right: Bumps work in the same way as embossing in a 2D paint program. In fact, if we run the Emboss filter on the bump map in Photoshop, we get exactly the same result as our 3D render.

Below: Here is a grayscale image, which can be used as a bump map.

Below center: Notice that light areas are rendered as raised bumps while areas that are dark are rendered as depressions.

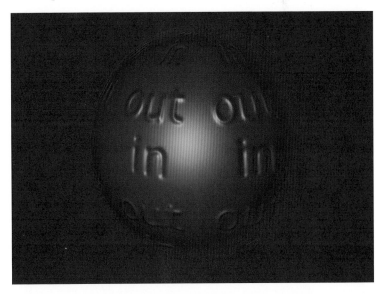

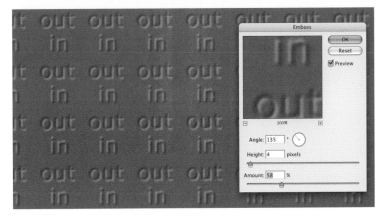

SHADERS The term "shader" is used in many different ways in 3D. In the broadest sense, a shader is any program or algorithm that does something to the process of rendering an image. The simplest kind of shader is one that produces a 2D pattern, such as a random fractal noise. On the surface it seems like a bitmap image, except that the pattern is generated at render time by the software.

Below left: **A 2D shader is like a bitmap texture. It needs to be mapped correctly to the object to which it is applied. Note that at the edges of the cube, the shader is stretched into streaks because the side faces are perpendicular to the shader's mapping projection.**

Below right: **A 3D shader permeates the object to which it is applied. Wherever the object's surface intersects the shader, you'll see the pattern without it smearing.**

Bottom left: **With a 3D shader, even if we take a gouge out of the object you will still see the pattern perfectly without signs of smearing. This is because the 3D texture is volumetric.**

Bottom right: **A volume shader applied to a light produces a 3D volumetric effect in the light's cone, as if there were smoke in the atmosphere.**

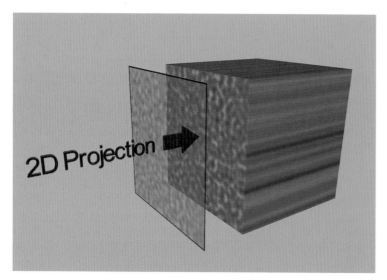

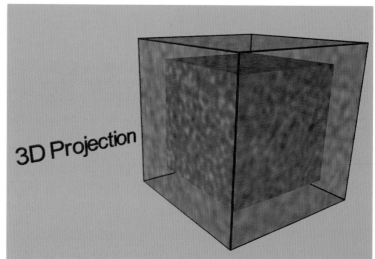

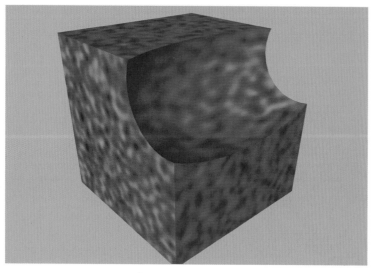

More complex shaders can create their patterns in 3D. These are often known as volume, or volumetric, shaders. To illustrate, imagine a cube with a 3D shader applied. If you cut the cube in half, the texture would continue all the way inside and appear on the cut surface. To all intents and purposes, a 3D shader is the same as a 2D shader, simply because in order to see the pattern you have to be rendering a surface, which is by definition 2D (topologically speaking). They differ in the way they are applied to objects. A 2D shader is just like a 2D bitmap; it needs to be properly mapped to an object or the pattern will stretch and smear. A 3D shader does not need explicit mapping because it literally pervades the space of the object—wherever the surface intersects the volume you'll see the shader's pattern.

A shader does not have to be limited to materials. There are shaders that modify the virtual camera to produce distortions that mimic real lenses. A Fisheye shader is a typical example. Other shaders are used to gather data to be used elsewhere. For example, a Fresnel shader calculates the angle between the camera and any given point on an object. This angle can then be used to modify a material channel. If the angle is small, it means that point on the surface is facing toward the camera. If the angle is large (up to a maximum of 90°), that part of the surface is facing away from the camera. Applying this kind of shader in a material's reflection channel produces the "Fresnel effect," whereby reflections appear weaker the more face-on we view a reflective object.

Other types of shader include true volumetric shaders that require no geometry to be applied to but render true volumetric effects in 3D space. A good example of this is volumetric light and fog.

Below left: **Viewed face-on, an object with a Fresnel shader applied in the reflection channel does not look very reflective. This mimics the behavior of real reflective surfaces as described by French mathematician Augustin Jean Fresnel (1788–1827).**

Below right: **As the surface-to-camera angle increases (measured perpendicularly to the object surface) the reflection becomes stronger and the surface color (diffuse color) gets weaker.**

Bottom and bottom right: **As the angle approaches 90° the reflection becomes very strong, obscuring the surface's actual texture or color.**

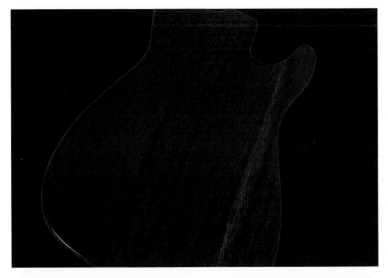

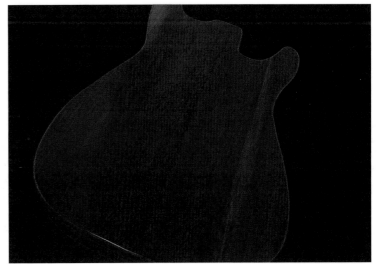

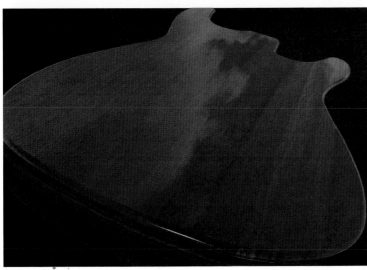

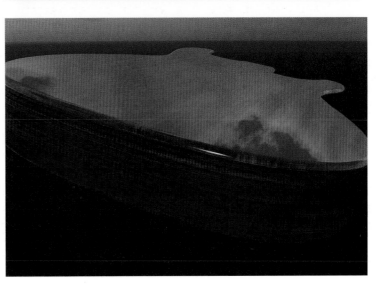

SHADOWS In everyday life we take shadows for granted—a fact so obvious that it might seem silly to state. In 3D, however, we can't take anything for granted, especially shadows. They play an integral role in the look of the final image, and without the right shadows any image, no matter how realistic otherwise, will appear fake. Real-life shadows occur naturally whenever a light source is obstructed by an object, but in 3D we have to make a lot of effort to get the same result.

There are two ways in which shadows can be created in a 3D program. One involves raytracing, and the other involves shadow maps. Raytracing is digitally analogous to the process at work in real life. Rays are cast into the scene, and when they hit an object they stop, resulting in a shadow behind the object where the ray would have ended. Raytraced shadows, however, always have hard edges, unlike what we see in real life illumination. With real shadows, as an object moves farther away from the surface onto which it is casting a shadow, the shadow becomes more and more fuzzy at the edges. Raytraced shadows do not produce this effect by default. However, soft raytraced shadows, also known as area shadows, can be calculated by sending out lots of extra rays and scattering them slightly. This technique does a good job of simulating soft edges and even re-creates the effect of increased fuzziness with distance that we see in reality.

Above right: **Normal raytraced shadows have hard edges. When objects are close to each other, this looks OK.**

Right: **When an object is far from the object receiving its shadow, the hard edges don't look quite right in comparison to what we expect to see in real life.**

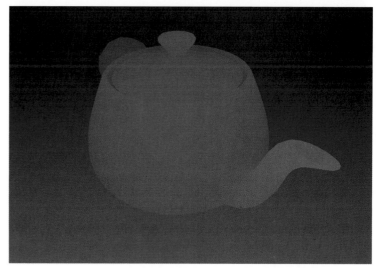

Top left: **With area shadows the raytracing technique is still used, except many more rays are cast and scattered slightly. When objects are close, you get a hard-edged shadow as you'd expect...**

Above left: ... but as the distance between objects increases the shadow becomes fuzzier, just as you would expect in real life. The problem is that area shadows take much longer to render because of all those extra rays.

Top right: **Depth-mapped shadows have soft edges as a matter of course. They are also fast to render, but unlike area shadows, do not become softer with distance.**

Above right: **You usually can't view the rendered Z-buffer directly in most 3D programs, but if you could, it would look something like this. Each pixel is given a value, depending on its distance to the light.**

Another way to make shadows in 3D is using depth maps. A depth map is a special render of the scene taken from the point of view of a light. In this render, sometimes called a depth-buffer or Z-buffer render, the distance of each point of an object's surface from the light is calculated. This information is then compared to a similar depth render taken from the camera. Without going too far into the technicalities, this enables the software to calculate what is and what is not in shadow. Because depth maps are rendered images, they can be blurred before rendering the final image to produce soft shadow edges. Also, because no raytracing is involved, depth-mapped shadows are very fast.

The downside is that their fuzziness does not alter with distance. However, this is often a less noticeable artifact than the hard edge of raytraced shadows, and so depth-mapped shadows are commonly used. As a simple rule of thumb, use depth-mapped shadows unless you have a good reason not to.

RADIOSITY 3D rendering has come on dramatically in recent years, especially in the area of photorealistic illumination. Normally when you render a scene, light strikes an object and that's it. The object's level of illumination is calculated, but its effect on the illumination of other objects in the scene is not.

In real life, light bounces off an object and strikes others in the immediate area. While this inter-object illumination is a common phenomenon in real life, it's very difficult to reproduce in 3D.

To do so, you need radiosity: a rendering technique that successfully calculates bounced light in a scene, and by and large accurately accounts for inter-object illumination. Radiosity works by spawning extra light rays when they hit a surface, sending them shooting off in all directions to

Above left: **Without radiosity a render can look very unnatural, with hard black areas and too much sharp contrast.**

Above right: **Using radiosity rendering, the same scene looks more organic and natural. Every nook and cranny is illuminated, and the secondary bounced light results in a softer, warmer, less computer-generated look. It's quite a dramatic difference. Notice too how color bleeding is also automatically generated in the process.**

see if they hit other objects in the scene. If they do, then those objects receive a little extra brightness. This secondary illumination also carries the color of the object, which is important for re-creating real-life appearances. This effect is known as color bleeding—you can see it in real life if you position a brightly colored object next to a white object (say, a red ball on a piece of plain paper); the color from one object spills onto the other.

Radiosity takes longer to calculate because of all the extra light rays produced. A quality setting in the radiosity section of a 3D renderer lets you control the effect, reducing the number of spawned rays for a faster, lower quality render for previews and tests.

Below: This is the same scene, but this time there are no lights as such. The illumination is created using a large self-luminous plane object. When rendered using radiosity, the bright surface of the plane acts as a light source illuminating the scene. This technique requires high quality radiosity settings to achieve the same results as normal 3D lights together with radiosity.

Below: The same technique can be used for exterior scenes. Using a large luminous "skydome" encompassing the scene you can create realistic ambient exterior illumination. Combine this with a normal distant light to simulate the sun, and you can create a good approximation of real-world outside lighting. In this example a blue material on the skydome simulates the diffuse blue light from the Earth's atmosphere, while the distant light provides direct illumination—here it's orange, to simulate a rising sun.

Currently many modern 3D programs offer adaptive radiosity technology that, like adaptive raytracing, reduces the rendering time by varying the quality of the radiosity algorithm over the image.

Because radiosity takes the brightness of surfaces into account when calculating scene illumination, it's possible to eliminate lights entirely. By making an object self-luminous, giving it a material with the Luminosity/Ambient channel set to full brightness, objects in the scene can act as light sources.

SUBSURFACE SCATTERING
Radiosity isn't the only advancement in rendering. While radiosity takes into account the light bounced between objects in a scene, subsurface scattering (SSS for short) deals with light that bounces around below an object's surface.

Many objects that seem opaque actually have a degree of translucency. Light can pass a fraction of an inch into the top layers of many materials and is scattered by the substance the object is made of, creating a degree of diffuse illumination below the surface of the object. Skin is a good example and one we are all familiar with. Hold a strong flashlight behind your fingers and you'll see a red glow, which gets brighter at the edges of your fingers. This is the effect that SSS replicates.

Even in normal lighting situations this scattered light beneath the surface affects the appearance of objects, and we can detect it. You only need to see a render from a 3D program that doesn't have SSS rendering features to see how true this is. When you want to create objects made from plastics, wax, quartz, and other diaphanous materials, subsurface scattering is absolutely essential. Even materials such as marble and other stones benefit from this effect. Trying to re-create even a simple glass of milk in 3D can prove fruitless without SSS rendering. However, like raytracing and radiosity, the intense calculations involved in subsurface scattering take time.

Below left: **A render of an object without subsurface scattering and with just two light sources, above and to the left of the object.**

Below right: **When *Subsurface Scattering* is turned on in the object's *Material*, a startling transformation occurs. The light permeates the volume of the object, giving it a semitranslucent appearance. This is an extreme example; SSS is just as effective when used subtly.**

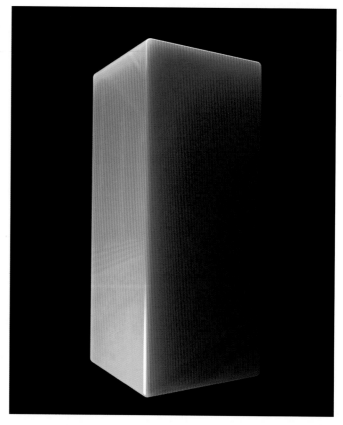

part 04. 3D core concepts

Left: Candle wax is a good example of a substance that scatters light and is translucent. With SSS enabled for the wax materials, the candle becomes more believable. Notice that a lot of the color of the wax comes through absorption of certain wavelengths of light; the color gets deeper, the farther in the light travels.

Below: Without SSS enabled, as in this image, the candle looks OK but the effect is not so realistic. The light and the surface don't react as we expect them to.

ARTIST'S TOOLKIT

05.01

PART 05. ARTIST'S TOOLKIT

CHAPTER ONE

ESSENTIAL TOOLS

To work in 3D, you need to have hardware that is up to the job. Luckily, that is no longer such a tall order. In the early days you would have spent thousands of dollars on Unix workstations and high-end software to equip yourself with a powerful 3D system. Now your average Mac or PC is more than up to the job.

Traditionally, the Apple Macintosh was not held in high regard in 3D circles. In part this was due to a lack of interest in the 3D market by Apple at the time, and because the Mac's operating system (the core software that controls the computer) was not modern enough for professional 3D work. As a result, few 3D programs were developed for the Mac. Although the Mac's enduring appeal for digital artists kept a small stock of exceptional 3D programs alive and kicking, Windows PCs took the lion's share of the 3D market. If you were serious about 3D, you bought a PC.

Things changed dramatically when Apple introduced its next-generation operating system, OS X. OS X was based on industry-standard Unix—the high-end 3D market's OS of choice—and this generated a huge revival in the Mac as a valid 3D platform. Now most of the high-end 3D programs have been ported to OS X, including the industry-leading Maya. Combined with Apple's latest G5-processor Power Macs, the Mac has everything going for it for 3D.

Windows PCs remain the bedrock of high-end 3D design, and on the whole are slightly cheaper. The bottom line for many artists, however, is that Microsoft's Windows XP operating system lags behind Apple's OS X in terms of ease of use and interface design. In these terms, the Mac wins hands down every time.

The other crucial thing for 3D work— or indeed any kind of graphics work—is the robustness of the OS. After years of producing one version of Windows for home users — Windows 95, 98, or ME—and one for professionals—Windows NT or 2000—Microsoft now has just one basic core, based on professional 32-bit NT kernel. As a result, both the Home and Professional versions of Windows XP have a solid foundation, and if you're not running either Windows 2000 or XP, you really should upgrade.

106   **part 05.artist's toolkit**

Similarly Apple's OS 9 will soon cease to be supported on new Macs, and it's not really suitable for 3D work anyway. Or rather, OS X is so much more advanced that it would be folly for your Mac not to run it. Any of the latest Macs, including the iMac G4, Powerbook G4, and Power Mac G5s, come with OS X already installed. Many older G3s can also run OS X, so it's worth upgrading these, too.

With XP and OS X you have protected memory, multiprocessor support, and pre-emptive multitasking. Although that sounds like technojargon, these are essential ingredients for a modern OS. With protected memory, for example, if one program crashes the system, all other programs will keep running. It's a fact of life that computer programs crash, so an OS that can protect your hard work from a system-wide lock is essential. Multiprocessing is also very useful because many computers, including some Apple Power Macs, feature multiple CPUs for faster performance.

In the end, however, the choice of Mac, PC, or Unix platforms is not purely determined by how powerful or affordable the computer is, or how good the OS is. If you're serious about 3D design, your choice of 3D program should be the first determiner, since not all 3D programs run on all operating systems. 3ds max, for example is Windows only, and Houdini is available only for Unix and Windows. Maya Unlimited is also not available for OS X, though Maya Complete (missing a few of the high-end features like cloth and fur) does run on the Mac platform.

Left: **Apple's OS X is based on industrial-strength Unix, yet is easy to use, fast, powerful, very robust, and gaining a lot of ground in the 3D industry. The perfect OS for 3D artists? Probably.**

Right: **If you want to take advantage of relatively cheap PC hardware and can live without the cool design of OS X, then Windows is the way to go.**

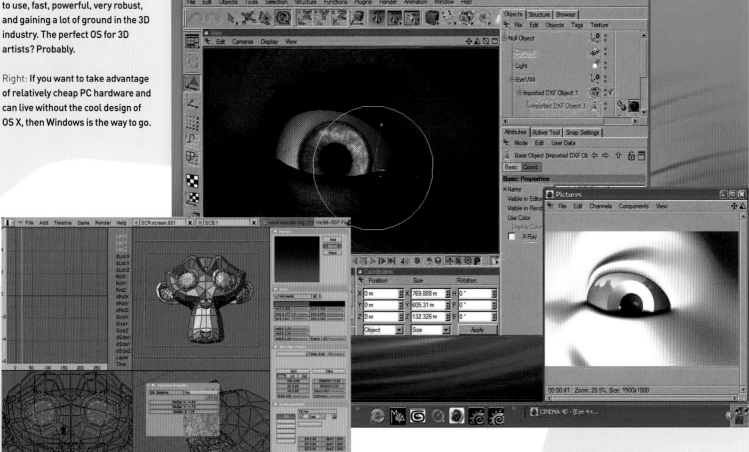

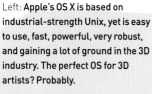

Left: **A free flavor of Unix, Linux is an open source operating system with many different incarnations, all based on the same core. It's very robust, but it doesn't have huge** support from 3D artists and is mainly used by large 3D facilities for networked rendering or by renegade tech-heads with a hatred of all things Microsoft.

WHAT YOU NEED TO DO 3D Once you've got past the basic question of OS, it's time to put a system together. 3D graphics is very CPU intensive, so it makes sense to get the fastest computer you can lay your hands on. If you are buying a machine specifically for 3D, you have the opportunity to create a system optimized for this demanding discipline, but most off-the-shelf PCs and Macs are perfectly suited to 3D work. These days, even some laptops can handle the workload.

Right: **Widescreen aspect ratio LCDs, such as the Apple Cinema Display, can support huge resolutions up to 1,680 x 1,050, giving you lots of space at the edge of the screen for command palettes and toolbars.**

Below: **CRT monitors are gradually being superseded by flat LCD screens. They are still widely used and a decent 19-inch CRT monitor can be purchased quite cheaply these days.**

Just make sure that you have enough RAM. For 3D work, 256Mb should be considered a minimum, 512Mb is highly recommended, and 1Gb of RAM isn't excessive.

Obviously, processor speed is important. If you're taking the Mac route, aim for a G5 processor if you can afford it, or as fast a G4 processor as you can manage if you can't. The graphics and memory subsystems are faster on the Power Mac systems than on their eMac or iMac equivalents, but the latter are still fast enough to work in 3D.

Left: A recordable DVD drive is a smart investment for 3D designers, enabling you to store and backup vast reams of complex textures and 3D data.

Below: If you want to become a professional 3D artist and work freelance, then think carefully about your work environment. One of these can make all the difference.

Finally, you're going to need a lot of storage space. In terms of hard disk space, consider 40Gb the minimum for notebooks and 80Gb the minimum for desktop systems. 120Gb or above would be a sensible choice. Likewise, some sort of backup is a must. Some people prefer an external hard drive, others prefer to burn work to CD using a built-in CD-RW drive, and as files get bigger a recordable/rewritable DVD drive looks more and more useful. In any case, it's a good idea to have something: there's nothing worse than losing all the data for a major project just before it's due for submission.

For a PC, aim for a Pentium 4 running at a minimum of 2.6GHz with Intel's speedy HyperThreading technology, or an AMD Athlon XP or Athlon 64 processor rated at 2.6GHz or above. Like the G5, the Athlon 64 is a 64-bit processor, which means it's ready for Microsoft's 64-bit desktop version of Windows XP, when it arrives.

We'll go into graphics cards on the next page, but one with 64Mb of texture RAM will work well. Look for 128Mb or more if you need to display a lot of textures in OpenGL at once.

Computer monitors are the next big concern, but don't necessarily think you need the biggest screen available to work efficiently in 3D. In professional desktop publishing (DTP) or graphics, where a monitor needs to be able to display entire double page spreads, 21-inch or 22-inch CRTs (Cathode Ray Tube screens) are commonplace. However, 3D work can be done on a much smaller screen space, and—believe it or not—the most popular choice for 3D artists is a 19-inch screen, closely followed by a 17-inch monitor. The benefit a small screen offers is a smaller footprint and affordability. A minimum of 1,024 x 786 resolution gives enough screen space for most 3D programs, though a 17-inch screen can be coaxed into running at 1,152 x 864, and 1,280 x 1,024 happily fits on most 19-inch screens without inducing eye strain.

LCD screens are an alternative to big, bulky, flickery CRTs, but are usually more expensive. The cost is coming down, however, and an LCD screen is ideal for 3D work, because it's flicker-free and much, much crisper. This reduces eye strain and fatigue.

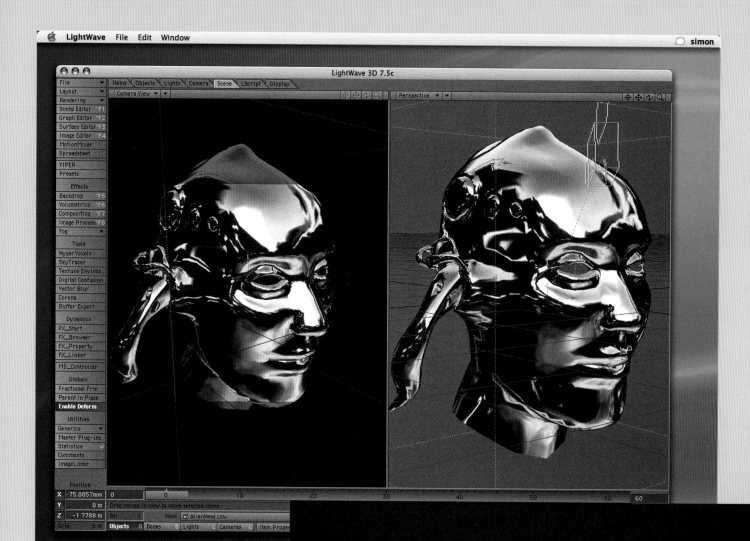

Above: **OpenGL is an API** (Application Program Interface) developed to help render 3D graphics quickly. A graphics card can work with a 3D program to speed its display as long as they both support OpenGL—they don't need be specially written to work together because they share an understanding of this common API.

Right: **Direct3D is another API for** display graphics. However, it's mainly used for in-game graphics on the Windows platform (and Microsoft's Xbox console) rather than digital content creation.

GRAPHICS CARDS AND APIS The graphics capabilities of a computer are an important consideration for 3D, as you might expect. There are two aspects to graphics hardware that can end up causing confusion, and a lot of this confusion is down to marketing.

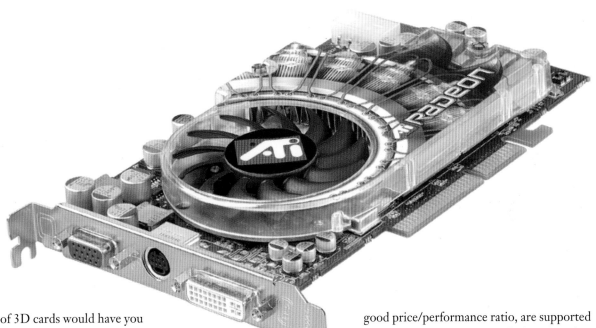

Despite what manufacturers of 3D cards would have you believe, the speed of the computer's CPU and the amount of RAM installed are still the most important factors in serious 3D graphics, because these affect how fast the 3D program runs and how fast it renders. The graphics card, or the 3D-accelerator card, is still important—it's just that it's not as important unless you're playing games.

When you're working in 3D graphics, the graphics card powers the display graphics, not the final render, so any impact it has is restricted to the speed at which a 3D program displays the 3D scene as a work in progress. That's still significant: working on a 3D scene does require interactivity, so the faster the graphics card, the faster the display and the faster you can work. However, this is not a linear relationship, and there comes a point where the speed of the card will have minimal effect on the work you can do.

Cutting-edge 3D cards will fetch a high premium, too, so in the long term, the money may be better spent on CPU power. Mid-range 3D cards aimed at pro 3D users, such as those from nVIDIA or ATI, are a good choice, and you should also look at less expensive, game-oriented cards. These offer a

Above: **A graphics card accelerates the display of the 3D graphics on your computer. Games-oriented cards are good options if you are on a budget and will usually work well with most 3D programs. nVIDIA or ATI-based cards are the safest bet. Both companies have good relationships with the major software developers, and both have universal drivers, which can be downloaded from the appropriate website.**

good price/performance ratio, are supported by solid drivers and are usually based on the same fundamental technology.

Macs don't have the kind of support from third-party graphics card manufacturers that PCs do, but cards using nVIDIA and ATI chipsets are available and are suitable for all but the most demanding 3D scenes.

The important thing to remember is that a graphics card will not make renders go faster—they only improve the interactivity of the 3D display while you model and work with surfaces. There are two main technologies used to power display graphics: Direct3D (part of Microsoft's DirectX API) and SGI's OpenGL. Direct 3D is the choice for Windows-based gaming, but OpenGL is the de-facto standard in professional 3D graphics. Whatever card you choose, it should have full OpenGL support if you intend to work in 3D.

PART 05. ARTIST'S TOOLKIT

CHAPTER TWO

SOFTWARE

3D software tends to range in complexity and sophistication, although these days even the simplest 3D software is capable of impressive results. However, choosing the right 3D program is not a trivial matter, nor is it an easy one. There are many factors to take into account, and your choice will also depend on your intentions. Do you just want to dabble or include a little 3D rendering in your website? Perhaps you are a 2D designer and want to start incorporating 3D in your illustration work. Maybe you have learned about 3D using free software and intend pursuing 3D as a career. Over the next few pages we'll look at the options available in three general sectors of the market: basic, intermediate, and advanced. Most 3D programs are available as demo versions, so you can try them out and get a feel of how they work before committing any cash.

SOFTWARE: BASIC

At the bottom end of the market there are plenty of low-cost, easy-to-use 3D programs. Because of the low cost and small market share, this is a volatile sector, with 3D apps popping into and out of existence like quantum foam. Some of these apps last a little longer than normal, while others vanish without trace, so don't be surprised if any mentioned here are no longer available by the time you read this. Whatever the name, they all tend to follow the same basic path—making 3D as easy as possible, but without the power and finesse of the more expensive packages.

Above: **If you want something for nothing, there are a few freeware versions of 3D packages available. 3D Canvas from amabilis.com is a cut-down version of the company's commercial 3D packages. It's a fully functional 3D app but is** **probably more suited to the intermediate 3D users or keen beginners. There is a lot of free Mac 3D software available, too, but these packages tend to be more intermediate or advanced in nature.**

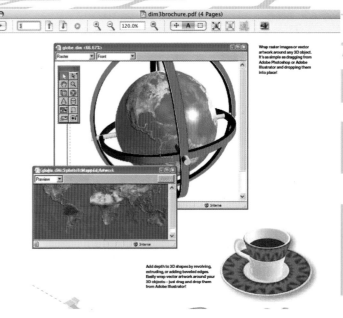

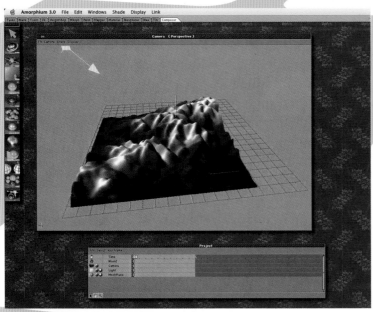

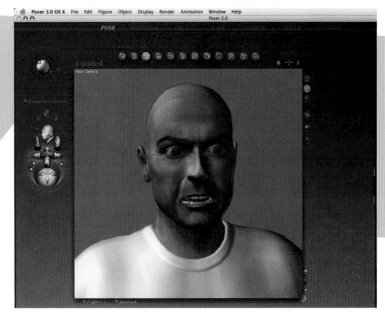

Top row, left to right: **Xara 3D is a** typical low-end 3D package, still going strong after multiple versions. Costing about $39, it's a PC-only 3D program that won't break the bank but is pretty limited as 3D programs go. Xara is great for quick logos and fun titles but that's really about it.

Adobe Dimensions is a plug-in for Illustrator (Mac or PC) that generates lit and rendered 3D objects from Illustrator curves and text. Again it's limited but very simple to use, and for some it's all that's needed.

Bottom row, left to right: **Although** more suited to intermediate users, Amorphium from ElectricImage Inc. is an easy-to-use 3D program designed to work in a very hands-on way. If you want to sculpt 3D objects as if they were lumps of clay then render them very simply, it's a good way to go.

Poser is included here because it is so easy to use, but in fact its usefulness extends right up to pro 3D work. It's a 3D character renderer and animator that lets you pose and animate ready-made, high-quality 3D figures. It's very powerful, but it's not an all-rounder: it does one thing only—but does it very well.

SOFTWARE: INTERMEDIATE

Intermediate 3D software can be classed as packages that don't attempt to simplify 3D, but which let you access all aspects of a scene, from building models from scratch, to creating and modifying lights and textures, and rendering full resolution images or animations. There are lots of programs to choose from here, and nearly all of them are good. Some of the more notable offerings are listed here as an example of what to expect for your money. These programs have all been around for a few years in various incarnations and should continue to be so for the near future.

Right: This is the core application that forms the hub of Maxon's advanced 3D system. It can be bought on its own without the advanced plug-ins, and as such represents a fantastic bargain. It features a powerful modeling system, animation, and fast rendering. It can be upgraded to the full advanced version simply by buying the plug-in modules.
www.maxon.net

Left: Strata's Strata 3D has a long history and is available for Mac and PC. It's a sturdy if slightly archaic 3D program, but it has found favor with many digital illustrators. It has some good rendering features, including radiosity, which are rare at the price.
www.strata3d.com

Opposite: Pixels is a Mac-only 3D program that offers advanced rendering and animation and robust modeling for a modest cost. It also features a renderer called Tempest based on the REYES algorithm—the same one used in Pixar's RenderMan software.
www.pixels3d.com

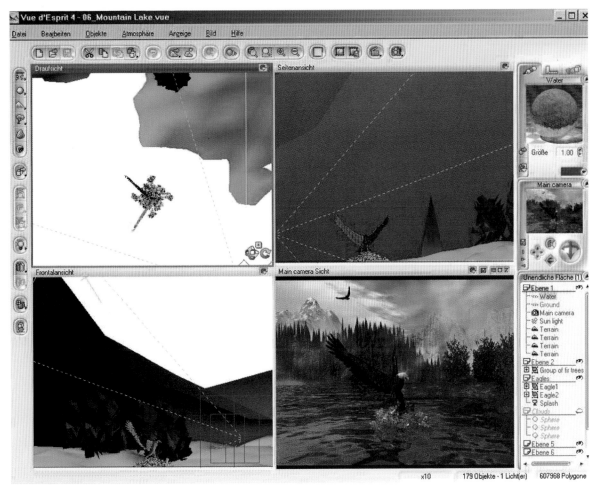

Left: Vue d'Esprit from e-on Software is a landscape creation and rendering program along the same lines a Corel's Bryce 3D. It's a lot more powerful, however, and can generate impressive trees, shrubs, and plants, too.
www.e-on.com.

Below: Corel's Bryce 3D is an interesting 3D program. It's primarily a landscape-rendering application, designed to produce skys, seas, and terrains in a very efficient way. It can be pressed into service as a more general-purpose 3D tool, too, but lacks any serious modeling tools.
www.corel.com

■ The quality of intermediate 3D software can vary, but there are a few things to bear in mind. Make sure the rendering is up to scratch, and examine on-line galleries of the software, which you can usually find on the developer's site. This will usually give you a good idea of the quality on offer. Most of the programs are available as demo versions so they can be downloaded for evaluation.

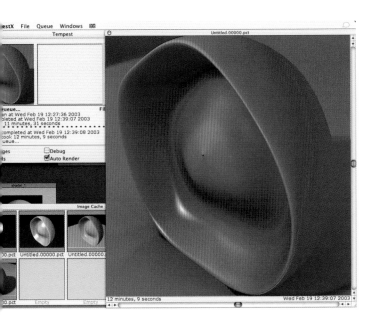

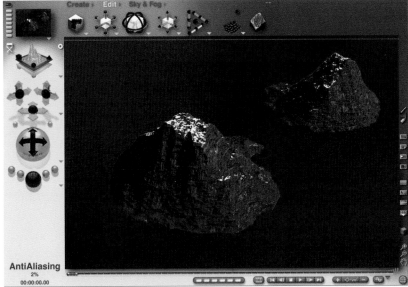

SOFTWARE: ADVANCED

In the upper echelons of 3D graphics software, there is a group of five or six packages that define the state of the art of commercial 3D software. These 3D packages cost upward of $1,000, and are full-featured 3D packages capable of creating anything you can imagine. Actually that's the wrong way to put it. The high-end 3D programs are sophisticated tool sets that give 3D artists the freedom to create anything they can imagine and do so efficiently and to tight deadlines.

The key features of these apps is that elusive and hard-to-define quality, workflow. 3D is such a complex discipline that the methodology used throughout a 3D program, and its interface and design, have as much impact on the work as the technological features and tools themselves do. At the high-end it's not so much the tools as their implementation that makes the difference, and each 3D app has its own style of working.

These high-end 3D programs include Softimage|XSI, Discreet's 3ds max, Side Effects' Houdini, Newtek's Lightwave 3D, Alias' Maya, and Maxon's Cinema 4D. There is another high-end package called PhotoRealistic RenderMan, which is a renderer, not a full software suite. However, RenderMan is arguably the most popular 3D renderer for high-end effects and is used together with the likes of Maya, XSI, and Houdini in movie and broadcast work. It's costly, seriously powerful, and runs on IRIX, Linux, and Windows operating systems, and has been announced for OS X as well.

Above: **Newtek's Lightwave 3D is a** dual application featuring separate modeler/texturing and animation/ lighting/rendering apps. Its quirky interface is deceptively powerful, and it offers one of the best quality renderers you could hope for. www.newtek.com

Below: **Discreet's 3ds max has always been a popular choice. Its design is not as modern as Maya or Softimage | XSI but it holds its own, especially in the games production market, and comes with Mental Ray rendering as standard.**

Right: **Houdini is a fully procedural animation system that takes the node-based architecture to the nth degree. Sublimely powerful it's not for the faint-hearted, but offers the kind of flexibility other apps only hint at.**

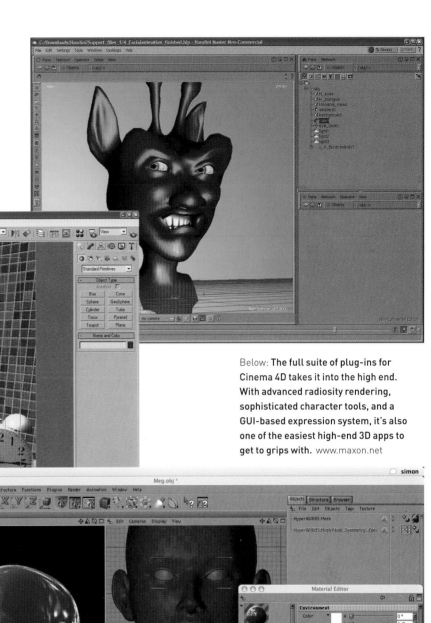

Below: **The full suite of plug-ins for Cinema 4D takes it into the high end. With advanced radiosity rendering, sophisticated character tools, and a GUI-based expression system, it's also one of the easiest high-end 3D apps to get to grips with.** www.maxon.net

Opposite above: **Softimage | XSI combines sublime modeling with nonlinear animation, scripting, and phenomenal rendering through tight integration with Mental Images' Mental Ray rendering software. It also features an integrated 2D/3D compositor.**

Opposite left: **Alias's Maya 3D software is extremely powerful. Its node-based architecture enables complex animation and rendering linkages to be created and it offers a nonlinear modeling history, plus Mental Ray rendering.**
www.alias.com

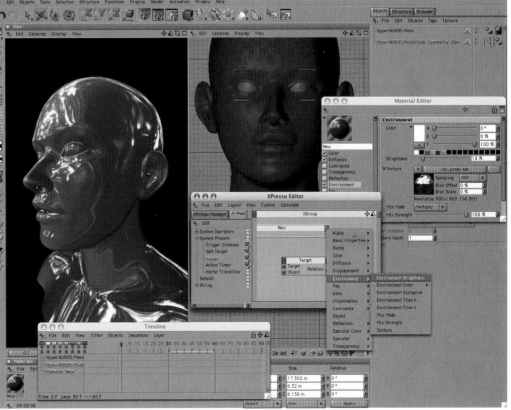

FREE SOFTWARE

FREE SOFTWARE The latest trend in the high-end 3D market is for the big 3D developers to offer free versions of their packages, slightly modified in some way so that they can't be used commercially. Alias, Softimage, and Side Effects Software all produce "experience" or "personal learning" versions of their high-end 3D apps. These let you see what it's like to use the latest cutting-edge 3D software for free.

The noncommercial safety features vary from program to program. Alias has the most severe in its version of Maya PLE. The OpenGL shaded display as well as any rendered images are emblazoned with Alias's logo and "commercial use prohibited by license" just in case you forgot. Maya PLE is not save-disabled but the file format is not compatible with the commercial version of Maya, preventing models from being created for free in PLE and opened in Maya commercial. XSI Experience has similar safety measures but they are less intrusive. The best deal is Houdini Apprentice, which has a tiny "not for commercial use" disclaimer in one corner of the screen and a custom file format.

Below left: **Maya PLE** is free to use noncommercially, but has severe watermarking. At least it gives you a taste of what the high-end is all about.

Below right: **XSI Experience** has minimal watermarking and is good for noncommercial use, although rendering size is restricted.

Demos and personal learning versions are one thing, but what can you get for free? Well, surprisingly there are plenty of free 3D programs available. So long as you realize that you're not going to get as slick a package as a commercial 3D app, they are well worth a look.

One of the best free 3D apps available is Blender. This program is a full 3D production package featuring the kinds of tools and functionality you'd expect to see in a mid to high-end application. The company that is now developing the program is a nonprofit organization, and as such Blender can be downloaded for free from www.blender3d.com. It's available on several platforms, too: Windows, OS X, Linux, Irix, Free BSD, and Sun Solaris.

Renderers are also pretty easy to come by, though many of these have been created by computing students and are usually command-line. Some free renderers include Lightflow (www.lightflowtech.com), Virtual Light (www.3dvirtualight.com), and Angle (www.dctsystems.co.uk). POV Ray is a famous free raytrace renderer, but it lacks an easy-to-use GUI.

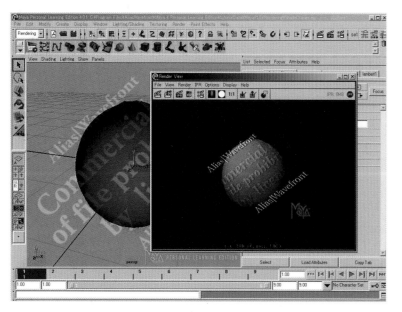

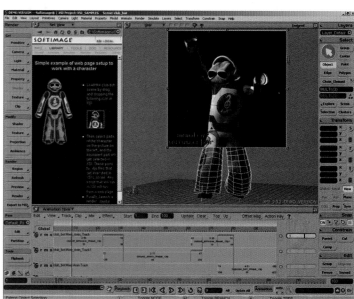

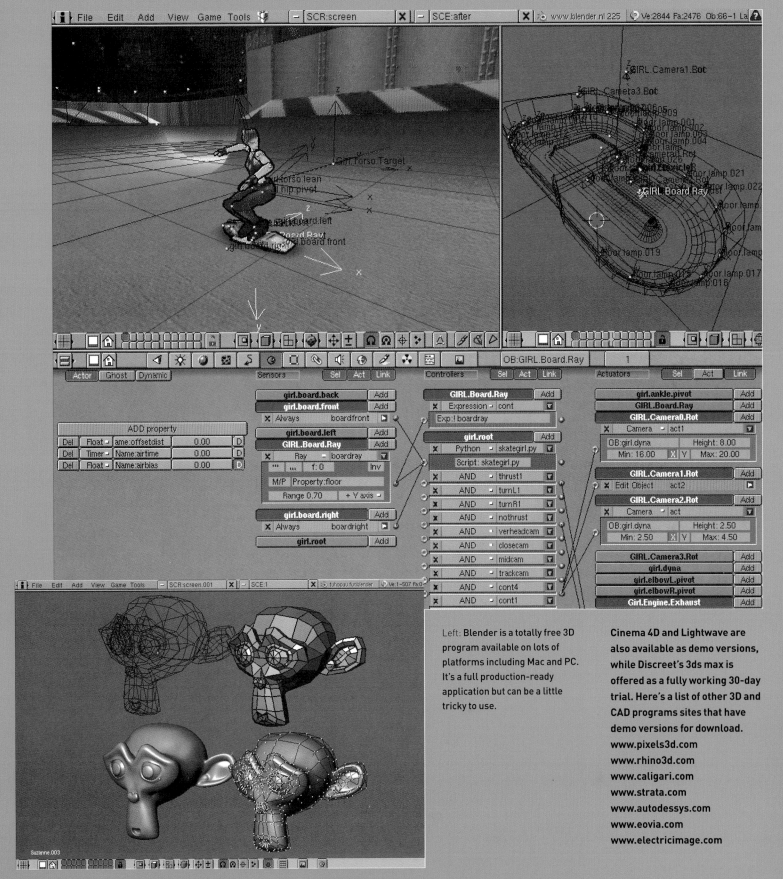

Left: Blender is a totally free 3D program available on lots of platforms including Mac and PC. It's a full production-ready application but can be a little tricky to use.

Cinema 4D and Lightwave are also available as demo versions, while Discreet's 3ds max is offered as a fully working 30-day trial. Here's a list of other 3D and CAD programs sites that have demo versions for download.

www.pixels3d.com

www.rhino3d.com

www.caligari.com

www.strata.com

www.autodessys.com

www.eovia.com

www.electricimage.com

3D PLUG-INS Many 3D programs are extensible via plug-ins. These may be made by the developer of the program and available as an optional extra, but more often than not, third-party developers create the bulk of plug-ins for a given 3D app.

Above: **Shave and a Haircut** is a hair rendering and simulation technology developed by Joe Alter but which is available as a plug-in for several different 3D programs. It's unusual since most plug-ins are developed for a specific 3D package.

Right: **Roofgen** is a plug-in for Cinema 4D that generates simple pitched roof beams. It's handy if you need to produce a lot of different buildings with interior roof details.

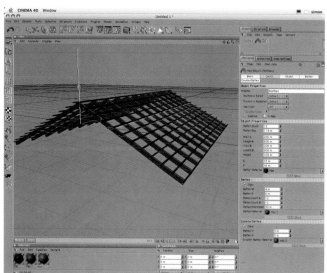

Most of the advanced 3D programs accept plug-ins, although you may have to buy them specifically for your chosen 3D package. As the ability to use plug-ins is less common with low-end and mid-range applications, you should always check before you buy. It's worthwhile spending a bit more in the long run on a 3D program that is extensible, because to some degree you future-proof your purchase.

If a program is popular, with a large user base, it's likely to have a healthy third-party plug-in community, too. Examples are Lightwave and 3ds max, both of which have thriving plug-in communities, and many of the plug-ins are available for free. Frequently, plug-ins tackle a very specific problem so may or may not be useful to you. Sometimes, however, there are free plug-ins that everyone wants, and the developer can gain a lot of kudos by providing them to the user base at large.

Plug-ins vary in nature and complexity and offer new functionality in many different areas of a 3D program. Some replace entire sections of a 3D program, such as Brazil r/s by Splutterfish. This is a commercial rendering engine that plugs into 3ds max to replace the standard one. For a plug-in such as this to be successful, it has to offer capabilities that the standard version of the program does not, and in this case Brazil does just that. Its advanced Global Illumination and Raytracing engine—among a host of other features—has made it a popular plug-in within the games, visualization, and movie-effects communities.

part 05. artist's toolkit

Below left: **Some plug-ins perform very specific tasks, such as this plug-in, Rounder, for Lightwave 3D. It automatically rounds points and edges—a deceptively simple but time-consuming task in 3D programs—making it a very useful little tool.**

Below: **Some plug-ins are supplied with the program when you buy it. In fact, some of the added features found in new releases are really third-party plug-ins that have been bundled with the main program. Maya 5, for example, has Mental Image's MentalRay renderer bundled with the program. Alias' Maya-to-MentalRay plug-in provides the necessary connection to the third-party renderer.**

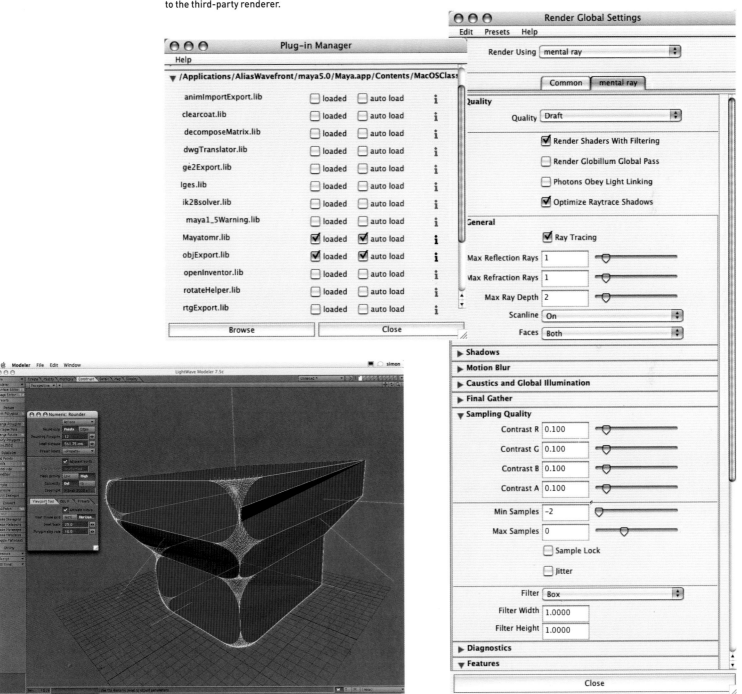

TEXTURE LIBRARIES You can never have too many textures. Texture maps come in all sizes, qualities, and resolutions. They may be hand-painted in Photoshop, or photographed, scanned, and imported (or acquired directly from a digital camera as is more common these days). Another way to get textures is to buy them from companies that produce royalty-free CD texture libraries. This is an easy way to expand your collection of textures and improve the quality of your models and renders. There is a wide variation in scope and quality, but you can usually download samples before you buy.

Left: **Dosch** is one of many companies that produce texture libraries on CD. It has a wide collection of subjects, including industrial and architectural materials and even HDRI images.

Below: **3dtextureworld.com** is a subscription site, but you gain access to hundreds of textures, and even a forum where you can request a texture if you need something specific.

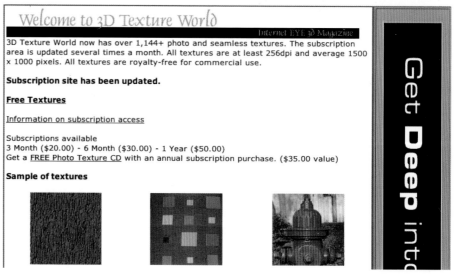

GET YOUR OWN TEXTURES

Don't forget that you already have a rich source of textures: the world outside. Get into the habit of using your digital camera to take photographs of interesting surfaces when you're out and about. Overcast days are the best, because textures work better without strong shadows cast on them, and you certainly don't want to see reflections or bright highlights either. Shoot your textures head-on to minimize distortion.

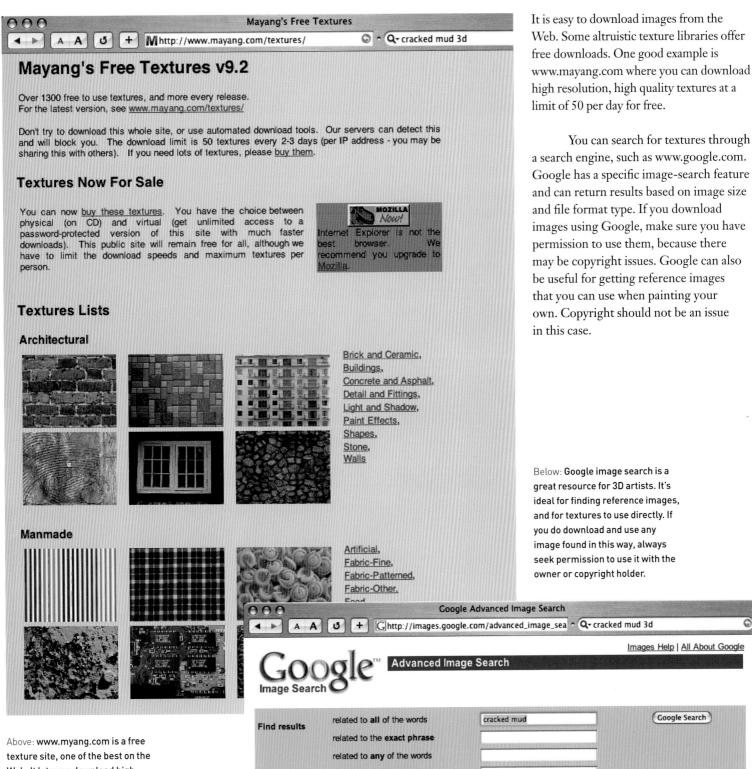

It is easy to download images from the Web. Some altruistic texture libraries offer free downloads. One good example is www.mayang.com where you can download high resolution, high quality textures at a limit of 50 per day for free.

You can search for textures through a search engine, such as www.google.com. Google has a specific image-search feature and can return results based on image size and file format type. If you download images using Google, make sure you have permission to use them, because there may be copyright issues. Google can also be useful for getting reference images that you can use when painting your own. Copyright should not be an issue in this case.

Below: **Google image search is a great resource for 3D artists. It's ideal for finding reference images, and for textures to use directly. If you do download and use any image found in this way, always seek permission to use it with the owner or copyright holder.**

Above: **www.myang.com is a free texture site, one of the best on the Web. It lets you download high quality 3D textures taken with a digital camera, although you can also buy the library on CD.**

Above left: A decent camera will achieve good results . Most cameras in the $250 bracket and higher will be suitable, and with prices always dropping it's wise to shop around.

Left: Resolution isn't as vital a consideration as it was. It's rare to get anything less than a 2-megapixel camera these days, which will create workable images of 1,600 x 1,200 pixels, while the current crop of 4-megapixel cameras can achieve 2,448 x 1,632 or more. Again the camera lens is the determining factor. Look for big names associated with film photography, and avoid buying a cheap camera just because it boasts a high resolution.

Above: This image was taken with a cheap digital camera. Notice the lack of focus and the darkening toward the edges of the frame. Even with a lot of work in Photoshop, this image would probably still not be worth using.

ANCILLARIES A number of useful gadgets come in handy for 3D work. Although not essential, the following ancillaries will make your life easier and your work more productive. These will help you build up a strong image library, which you can use for reference and also include in your 3D designs.

The digital camera is the most obvious tool to add to your workstation. Apart from grabbing textures, you can also use it to take photographs as reference for modeling, lighting, or texture, and to create environmental reflection maps and backdrops (e.g. skyscapes that work well in 3D).

When choosing a digital camera, buy the best you can afford. Just because it is "digital" does not guarantee great results, and the least expensive models on the market are likely to be unsuitable. Cheap digital cameras may suffer from excessive noise, poor lenses, and weak flash illumination. When capturing flat surfaces as texture maps, you want the most even image possible, so a camera that gives you images that get darker toward the edges is not any good.

Scanners used to be essential, but these days, digital cameras reduce the need to scan photographic prints or negatives. However, a scanner can be useful for scanning objects for textures that would be difficult to capture using a digital camera. The reason is light. In a scanner, the light moves with the scanning head, giving even illumination. This makes flatbed scanners more suitable for capturing textures such as crumpled paper, fabric, and other surfaces with a fine detail.

Another optional extra is a graphics tablet. This is not essential for 3D work, but it can be useful for 3D applications that have brush-based tools, and of course for creating custom textures in Photoshop. Artists who like to use graphics tablets usually swear by them and even end up using them in place of a mouse.

Finally, you will need an Internet connection. Apart from catching up with the latest 3D news, downloading patches and updates for your software and operating system, an Internet connection is handy for gleaning inspiration, reference images, and 3D models from around the net. A dial-up connection is OK but if you can access broadband in your area, it should be high on your list of priorities.

Below: **A scanner is not essential, but it can be useful for scanning certain objects and textures. One benefit is that the image will have an even brightness with no shadows—perfect for 3D.**

INTERNET RESOURCES The Internet is a fantastic resource for the 3D artist. There are countless websites around the world dedicated to the subject, offering tips and advice and even 3D models, meshes, and textures that you can download and use. A number of well known websites are dedicated to news and current 3D trends, and a vast number of individual home sites provide 3D eye candy galore. Some of these Web galleries are truly inspiring and well worth a visit.

A number of commercial websites sell 3D content. This is great if you are in a hurry and need a model quickly. One such site is TurboSquid.com. This is a well-organized 3D marketplace where you can browse and purchase 3D models, textures, materials, and scene files for all of the major 3D packages. The great thing about TurboSquid is that you can also sell on the site. Just upload any spare models you have, and they will be added to the library for sale. TurboSquid takes roughly 50% of the sales price, but if you have already built models, it's a good way to earn some extra on the side for little effort.

Below: www.turbosquid.com is a unique 3D vending site because it lets anyone upload and sell their models as well as buy them. You can even set your price. TurboSquid takes a cut, collects the payment, and pays you a royalty.

OTHER GOOD 3D SITES:
www.flay.com
www.xsibase.com
www.highend3d.com
www.3dluvr.com
www.3dring.org
www.postforum.com
www.3dlinks.com
www.3dpalace.com
www.3dspline.com

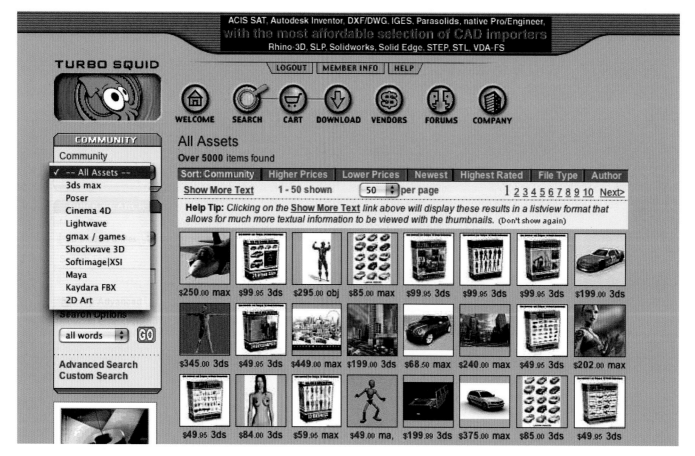

Top: www.cgchannel.com is a great pro-oriented 3D site featuring daily news updates, interesting feature stories, galleries, forums, and more.

Above: www.3dtotal.com is another news and features site, which runs along the same lines as cgchannel. It has some useful forums and tutorials, too.

Top: www.3dark.com is a good starting point for newcomers to 3D graphics. It features links to downloadable content, tutorials, and much more.

Above: 3DBuzz.com is a tutorial site that supports most of the top 3D programs. It offers free training and even used to send out free CDs with tutorial videos to anyone who asked.

3D TECHNIQUES
& DESIGN

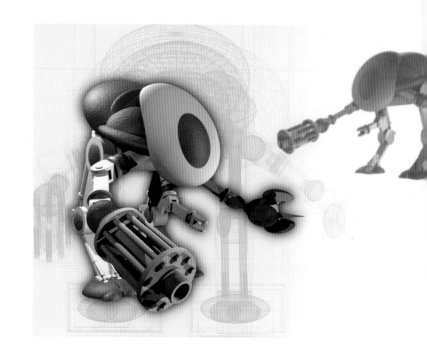

06.01

PART 06. 3D TECHNIQUES & DESIGN

CHAPTER ONE

TECHNIQUES

PRIMITIVE MODELING is the simplest kind of 3D modeling because it does not involve any complicated 3D processes or tools. It's a lot like building with a child's wooden blocks because you assemble a number of primitive objects into the desired shape. However unlike wooden blocks, you can scale and stretch the 3D primitives so that they more closely match the object you are trying to produce.

The primitives themselves are the standard, ready-made shapes that come with almost all 3D programs. These include the Sphere, Cube, Plane, Torus, Cone, and Pyramid, although some apps may have fewer or more primitives as standard.

The only tools you will use for this kind of modeling are the transformation tools: Move, Rotate, and Scale. To make a table, for example, you might use five cubes. The first cube is scaled along two axes parallel to the ground plane (XY or XZ, depending whether the 3D program uses Z or Y as the up axis) to make the table top. Then each of the other four cubes are scaled in Y (or Z) to make the legs. Each of the four legs can be positioned using the Move tool so that they lie below the table top cube at its four corners.

Above: **Some 3D programs such as Bryce only allow modeling using primitives. However, you can create very complex models using this method. This model was made entirely in Bryce, except for one or two Boolean operations. The shapes are standard primitives.**

part 06. 3D techniques & design

Below: A simple 3D table might be made from five scaled cubes. It's not very accurate, but what do you expect for less than a minute's work!

Bottom: **More detail can be added to this table using further primitive modeling. Because these cubes are parametric primitives, we can edit their settings to add some edge rounding to them. Another cube is added, scaled, and moved below the table top to make the frame. Even this minor detail makes a lot of difference to the appearance of the object, which looks much more solid.**

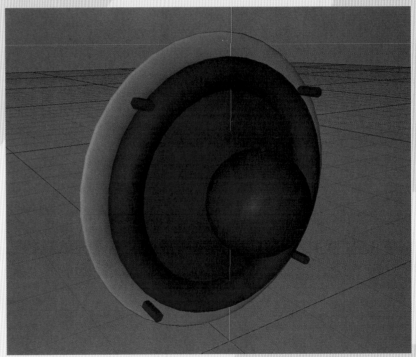

Above: **Here's another object made entirely using primitives. Some tricks can help make the most of this method of modeling objects. For example, the bolts are made using cylinders, except the number of sides has been reduced to 6 and smoothing has been turned off. A look around the back shows the object is really just an assemblage of 3D primitives.**

CURVES AND LINES Curves are special kinds of objects in 3D. They don't actually render but are instead used in the modeling process. Like curves in 2D drawing program 3D curves can be created to make open or closed shapes. You then use a further 3D operation—such as Extrude—on the curve to turn it into a renderable 3D object.

There are different types of curve depending on the kind of 3D program you are using. The most common types are Bezier and NURBS. Bezier curves work just like vector paths in a 2D drawing app, except that their points can lie anywhere in 3D space. The curve passes through its points, which also have Bezier handles that let you change the curvature of the curve. NURBS curves are a little harder to get used to because the curve does not pass through its points, except at the very ends. The points can be moved to influence the shape of the path, but this can be tricky as the points have to lie quite a way past the shape's boundary.

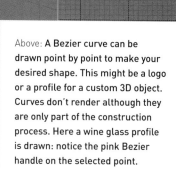

Above: **A Bezier curve can be drawn point by point to make your desired shape. This might be a logo or a profile for a custom 3D object. Curves don't render although they are only part of the construction process. Here a wine glass profile is drawn: notice the pink Bezier handle on the selected point.**

Left: **Only half the wineglass has been drawn because the curve will be used in a lathing operation, which rotates the curve 360° around a central axis to make the 3D surface.**

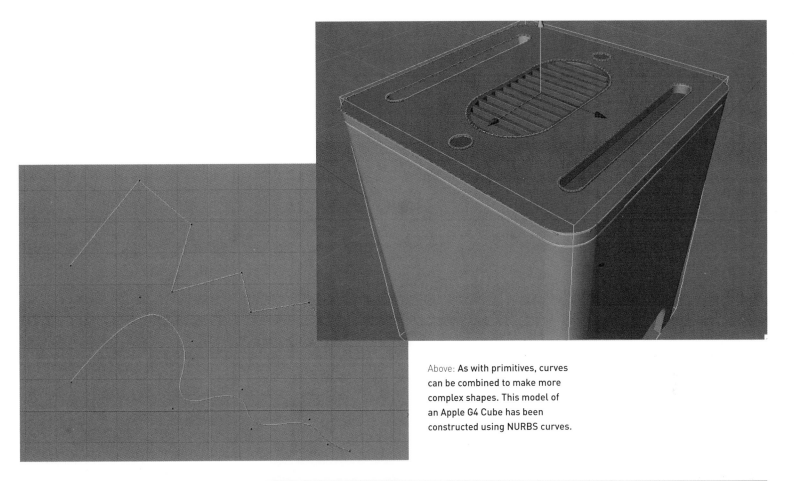

Above: **As with primitives, curves can be combined to make more complex shapes. This model of an Apple G4 Cube has been constructed using NURBS curves.**

Above: **A NURBS curve looks different to a Bezier curve. Except for the end points, its points, known as control vertices, do not lie on the curve itself. The only case where this is not true is in a linear NURBS curve (top).**

Right: **A NURBS curve can be used in exactly the same way as a Bezier curve, although they have different controls for their points and slightly different behaviors. Which type you use depends on your 3D app (you may not have a choice) and personal preference. In this example, two curves are combined in a *Sweep* operation.**

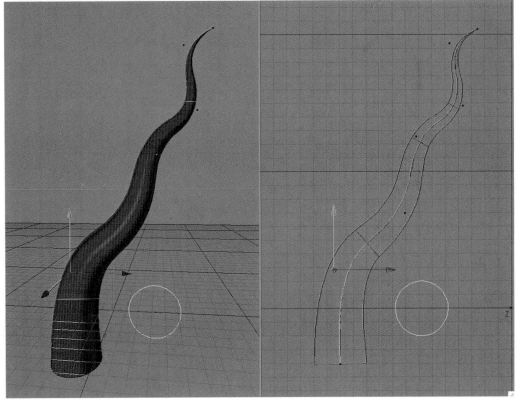

BOX MODELING Generating specific 3D forms can be done by using primitives as building blocks, or by combining curves and specific modeling operations such as Extrude, Lathe, Sweep, and Loft. However, you can also take a simple primitive object and model it directly by editing the points and polygons to get the desired shape you want.

Box modeling is the process of refining a simple primitive object, extending it and editing its components to make a more complex form. Beginning with a cube the points and polygons are edited until the final form is reached. In this example the model is being created as a low-resolution cage; the last step involves smoothing the cage to make a higher-resolution object.

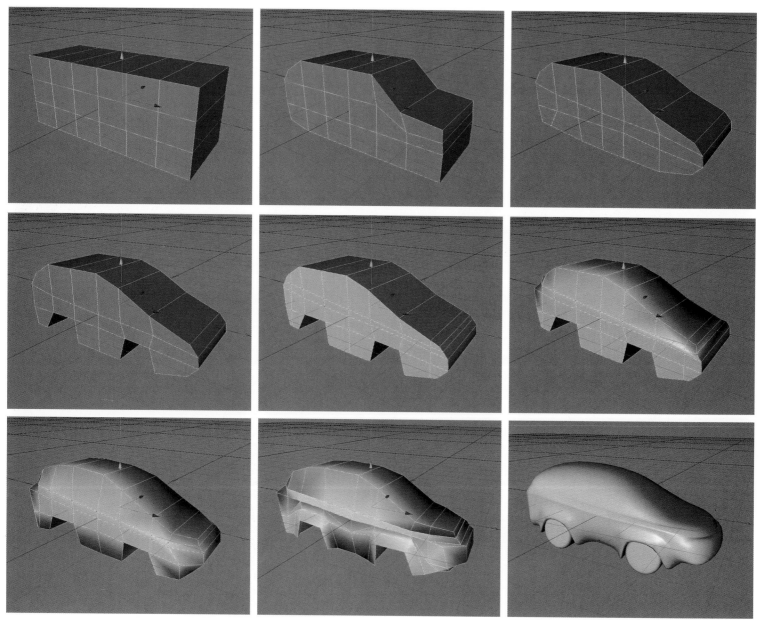

Polygons can usually be extruded and transformed using a specific set of polygon tools to let you extend the geometry of a simpler form into a more complex one. This is commonly called box-modeling because the starting point is often a cube (the box), although you could begin with any primitive that suits your purpose.

SMOOTHING AND SUBDIVISION SURFACES

Creating a high-resolution, smooth surface by box modeling would be painfully difficult if it weren't for smoothing algorithms. Smoothing (which is different from smooth shading) converts a low-resolution object into a high-resolution object by subdividing the polygons. Unlike normal subdivision, which doesn't alter the shape of the object, smoothing softens and rounds off the sharp edges of an object, making sure that the surface is smooth and continuous. Therefore when box modeling an object, the 3D artist bears in mind that it will shrink slightly and become less angular when smoothed. It's possible to check the effect by periodically applying smoothing, then undoing it.

A better alternative to smoothing is subdivision surface modeling. This employs the same technique as polygonal box modeling, but smoothing is continuously applied to the low-resolution cage. The artist can continue modeling the cage polygons while viewing the smooth surface below.

Below: **A typical use for subdivision surfaces is in 3D character modeling. This method is perfect for this kind of work because it generates single-skin, smooth, organic objects that deform well when animated.**

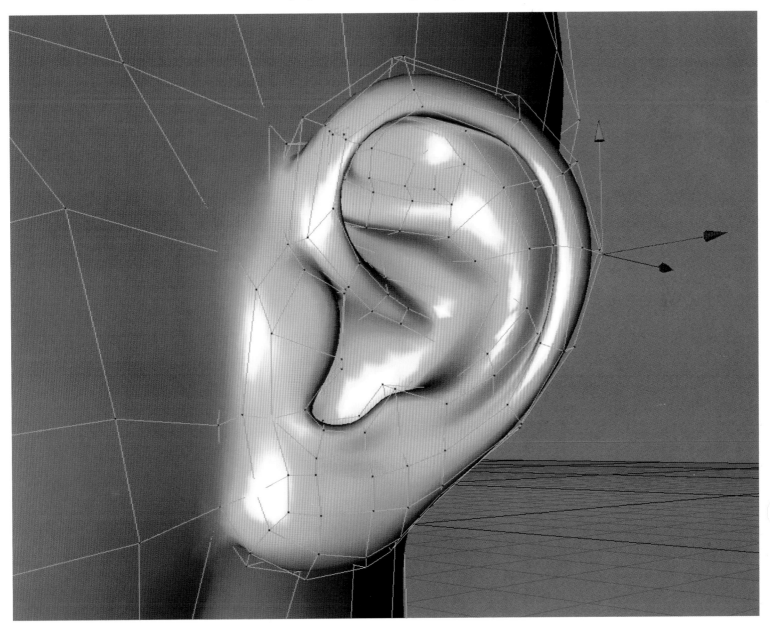

BOOLEANS

BOOLEANS Boolean modeling involves cutting away portions of one object using another—a working method that can be tricky to imagine because there is nothing analogous to it in the real world. Booleans are often the only way to accomplish certain shapes and details without resorting to building an object polygon by polygon.

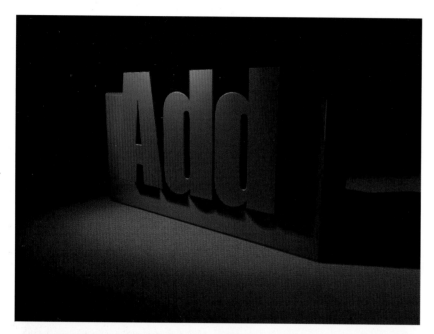

Booleans also have their problems, and their use is often avoided in polygon-based modeling programs. If they are used, it is at the end of a chain of modeling events rather than at the beginning.

In many solid modeling programs, Booleans are less problematic: the resulting object is usually as easy to edit as it was before the Boolean. Note, however, that NURBS cannot be Booleaned. While some NURBS programs (such as Maya) use the term Boolean for a modeling procedure, they are really using a different process known as trimming.

Left above: There are three main types of Boolean operation: Add, Subtract, and Intersect. Add combines two 3D objects into one object and discards any overlapping portions. Bear in mind that the process irrevocably alters the object's geometry. Externally no change is visible, but the effect is apparent if viewed from the inside or the object is given a transparent material.

Left below: The objects on the left have not been joined using Boolean addition, while the object on the right has been. When raytrace rendered using transparent materials, you can see the difference. Not only can you see the parts of the word "add" inside the block on the left object, but the refraction is different because the raytracer computes the ray as it travels through several objects. Each object intersection causes a refraction. On the Booleaned object, there are fewer refractions because it is a single solid object.

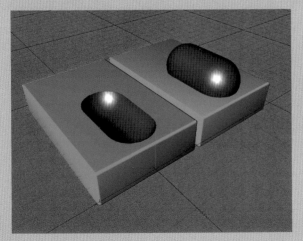

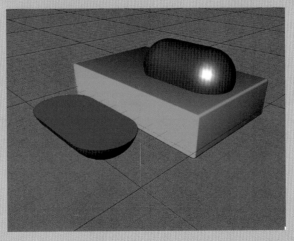

Above: **Intersections provide some interesting effects, such as here where a scaled cube and a head object are intersected to create slices through the head. The cube's translation can be animated to "build up" the head progressively.**

Far left: **Boolean subtraction removes the overlapping portion of one object from another. In this example a capsule is subtracted from a rounded cube. Notice that the material of the capsule is also left behind in the operation.**

Left: **The same objects but using Boolean Intersection. The overlapping portions of both objects are all that remain; the rest of the object geometry is removed.**

CHARACTER MODELING Character modeling can be thought of as a class of modeling in its own right. Creating a 3D character can be very challenging and requires a lot of trial and error, especially if the 3D character is to be animated.

What is classed a "character" varies. In animation, just about any object can be given character and made to seem alive, whether it's a teapot, a desk lamp (as in Pixar's *Luxo, Jr.* short film), or a stick figure. However as 3D graphics have progressed, realistic human 3D characters and caricatures have become more common. These 3D models have limbs and detailed facial features, modeled with a fine degree of detail.

When tackling such a model, a good 3D character artist takes great pains not only to make the model look good, but also to deform well. It's relatively easy to build a face using polygon or NURBs modeling tools, but there is a great deal of difference between a face that has been built with animation in mind and one that has not. It's all to do with surface topology—the way that the contours of the geometry are laid out over the face. In the quest to create good 3D faces for animation characters, modelers will often study human anatomy. It helps, for example, to make the surface geometry match the muscle structures under the skin. When parts of the face are animated, the bulges and creases form in the same way as they do on a real person's face.

NURBS can be used to create characters, but there are some limitations of this geometry type. To start with, the topology of a face is difficult to match using a single parametized NURBS surface. For one thing, a face has numerous holes (mouth, eyes, nostrils) and holes are one thing that a surface cannot have. One way around this is to create a face, starting with a sphere, making the pole of the sphere the mouth cavity, and sculpting the face by adding isoparms where needed. This mouth-centered method is good, but it produces a bunching of isoparms at the bridge of the nose.

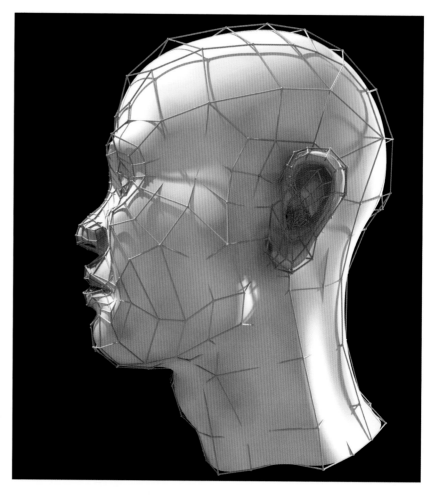

Another method involves stitching multiple NURBS patches together. Using stitching you can have NURBS surfaces that have holes in them. They are not really holes but gaps in the patchwork where a NURBS patch has been left out. The downside is that stitched surfaces rely on the 3D program to monitor the surface continuity continuously, which can make them slow to animate.

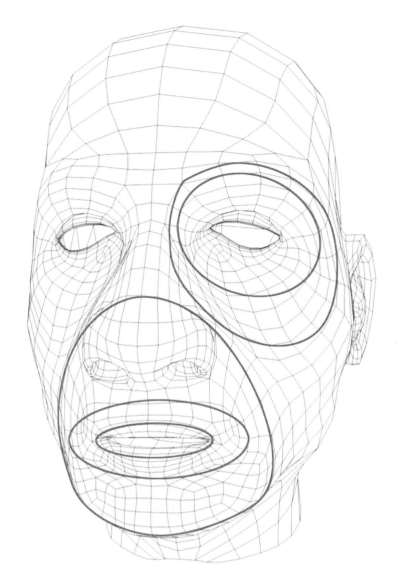

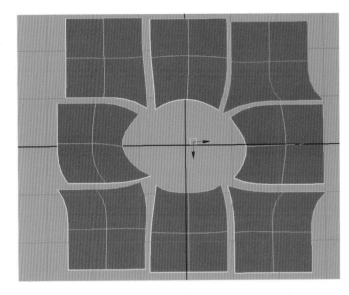

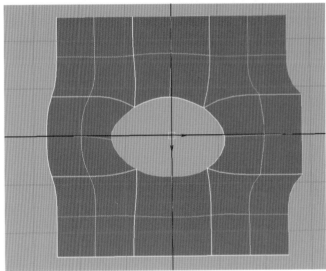

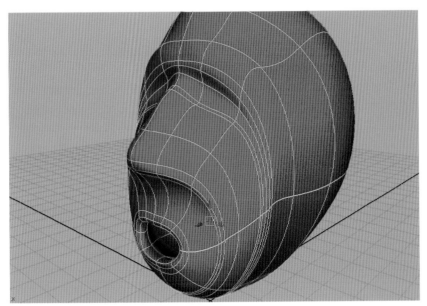

Above left: **In this model the geometry forms concentric circles around the mouth and eyes. This is a common technique for building human faces because it mimics the muscle structures in a real face. This helps the model deform more realistically when animated.**

Left: **The beginnings of a mouth-centered NURBS head. As you can see from the distribution of isoparms, this method is not ideal—it's wasteful and produces excessive geometry in certain areas.**

Above: **Holes can be created in NURBS models by creating a surface from multiple NURBS patches. The 3D software stitches the patches together to make it look like a seamless surface. This technique can be used to create the holes in a 3D character's face, such as the eyes or mouth.**

SUB-D CHARACTER MODELING Polygons are well suited to character modeling because they are easy to work with, support arbitrary topology, and combined with smoothing algorithms provide resolution independence. While it is possible to create the final resolution surface of a character from polygons, it is more usual to use a form of subdivision surface modeling. This lets 3D artists work with the absolute bare minimum geometry to make editing easy while producing a perfectly smooth surface when rendered.

Subdivision surfaces come in many guises. True subdivision surfaces have a hierarchical structure and, despite some similarities to polygons, are actually quite different. There are only a few programs that employ true hierarchical subdivision surfaces, Maya being one of them.

Other programs use a different method. This is the polygon proxy method, which goes by various different monikers including SubPatches, HyperNURBS, and MetaNURBS (although these have nothing to do with NURBS). With the polygon proxy method, the base mesh is a normal polygon model, which can be edited and refined in the normal way using regular polygon modeling tools. There is no local hierarchical refinement but that's not usually a problem.

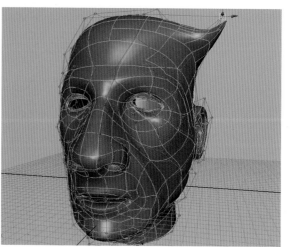

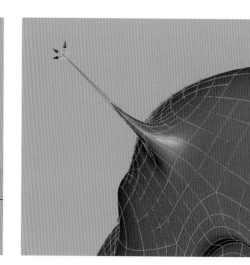

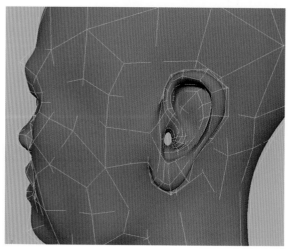

Top left: Maya's subdivision surfaces are hierarchical and follow the standard developed by Pixar. They let artists use a coarse base mesh as a cage that subtends a smoother surface beneath. This is much like other polygon smoothing methods.

Top right: Hierarchical subdivision surfaces let you progressively refine specific areas of a model, adding more detail where it is required, and only there. Here two levels of subdivision refinement have been added to create a demonlike horn.

Bottom left: You can step backward through the subdivision levels and edit the base mesh again. Even the region that has been refined still has its base polygon intact. This can be edited to modify the position of the refined horn farther up the hierarchy.

Bottom right: Ears can be tricky areas to model as they are an area of high detail attached to an area of very low detail. Because of this ears are often modeled separately and then attached to the head model. Using polygons, it's possible to join the ear to the head in such a way that you effectively reduce the geometry at the join to allow a smooth, seamless graft.

CHARACTER GEOMETRY

When it comes to building realistic 3D characters, the topology of the mesh is absolutely crucial if the character is to be animated. For cartoonish characters with rigidly jointed limbs, this is not important since the model will not be animated using deformations; rather each joint will pivot at the joint. For realistic character animation the model usually needs to be built as a single skin (one single net of polygons for the entire body surface).

Single-skin characters have no joints, and the arms, legs, shoulders, etc., are bent using a skeleton of joint deformers inside the model. In order that the mesh deforms correctly, you could simply have the mesh at a massive resolution. However, this would cause all sorts of other problems and would slow down the animation. It's far better to design the mesh properly so that deformations look natural and the model stays light.

Designing proper edge loops is one way to create good character deformation, but you'll probably find it difficult to get a mesh to flow in the way you'd like if you're new to this kind of modeling. One key aspect is to make sure that the model consists of quads only, at least those parts of the mesh that will deform greatly. A quad is simply a four-sided polygon, and this comes with two benefits: first, renderers like quads; and second, quads tend to subdivide better. Most subdivision surface algorithms support triangles and quads, and even N-gons (polygons with more than four sides), but the difference is that Quads seem to subdivide without causing problems. Triangles are okay in some places, not in others, and to be fair, using them is sometimes unavoidable. N-gons, however, are a definite no-no.

When working with a mesh you'll begin to see all the different ways that quads can be connected. Here are some examples you'll come across, and also some special topological devices that will help you when modeling.

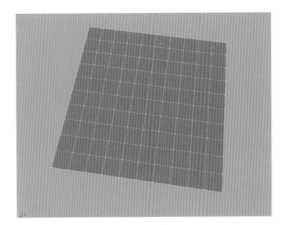

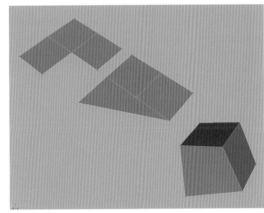

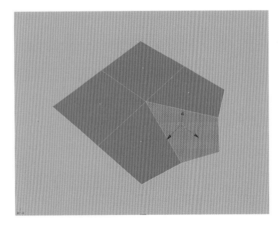

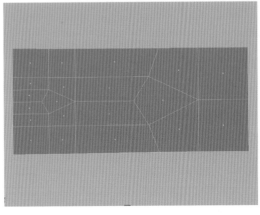

Left, top down: The most common topological pattern for quads is the regular grid. A grid deforms nicely and is topologically very sound. Note that each vertex is connected to four polygons (apart from those at the edges).

Another common topological structure is formed when a vertex is connected to three quads instead of four. This image shows a sequence converting a regular grid of polygons into a junction of three. Take a grid of four quads, delete one, then merge the remaining two vertices. The two groups of polygons on the right are identical, the far right one has been edited into a 3D form to show the junction better. Note that this three-way connection is the same as the corner of a cube and is a useful way to reduce the resolution of the mesh in specific areas or to create branching loops.

The opposite of the three-way junction is where you add rather than remove a polygon to create a vertex that connects to five quads. Count the edges—they are all quads. The selected polygon is one that has been created between the ones either side in this regular grid.

Five-way junctions are very useful for increasing the resolution of a mesh. In this example we begin with only two polygons on the right but as the mesh progresses toward the left, the resolution increases until we have six polygons. Two five-way junctions have been used to produce the increase in resolution while maintaining all-quads in the mesh.

PARTICLE EFFECTS Particles are a special kind of 3D object. With a polygon or NURBS model you want to keep the individual components together in one nicely built object, but with particles you want them to spray out all over the place.

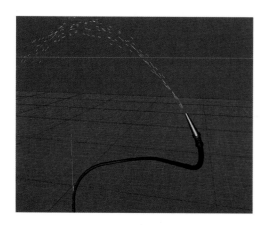

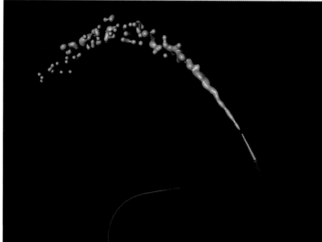

Far left: **Particles emitted from the end of a hose can be used to simulate a spray of water. However the particles themselves are just points in space. When rendered you won't see any particle effect at all.**

Left above: **In order to create a water effect you need to tell the 3D software what to do. In this case we apply a Metaballs geometry to the particle stream, which generates a blobby surface around each particle point and mingles with surrounding blobs. That's the geometry sorted out, but you still need to texture the object as you would any other.**

Left below: **Applying a custom water material to the blobby object finishes the effect. This water utilizes transparency with refraction, an environmental reflection map, and a bump map. The water is animated because of the emitter so a new surface is generated at each frame, creating the illusion of spraying water.**

Particles are used for all kinds of effects, particularly in movies and television, where they're used to create explosions, smoke, fire, liquids, and other volumetric substances.

To create particles you generally start with an emitter—an object that emits particles at a certain rate and direction. A typical emitter would produce a fountain effect where particles are sprayed upward in a cone, spreading out as they go. If the particles are set to react to gravity, they fall back down once their initial impulse has worn off. You could connect an emitter to the end of a hose object and animate the hose flaying around. The emitter would shoot particles into the scene as it moves, creating the effect of water spraying from the end of the hose.

You don't have to use an emitter to create particles. Objects themselves can be defined as particle emitters. When this is the case, particles are emitted from the surface of the object—either from the vertices or the polygons or randomly. The surface normals are used to define the direction of each particle so that the emission follows the shape of the object.

Right: **This star object has been set to emit particles from its surface. As the star moves, the particles fly off in all directions and, when rendered using the appropriate shader settings, creates a glowing shower of sparks that float in its wake.**

Top left: **Here's a simple volumetric fire and smoke shader attached to a particle emitter. Each particle is rendered as a true volume. The overlapping particles combine to look brighter, and each particle ages over time, becoming less red and bright as it turns to smoke.**

Top right: **A smoke shader is similar except that it's less bright and has no color. Note that the volumetric object can even cast shadows in the scene.**

Above: **The density of the volume has a great effect over the look of the particle cloud. Some materials, such as dust or snow, can appear dense in certain circumstances. Pyroclastic plumes from a volcano, or avalanches, are good examples. In this case the volume is very thick, and the surface casts and receives shadows. This is key to achieving certain smoke and plume effects.**

WHERE THERE'S SMOKE...

Particles systems are often used to create smoke and fire because there's usually no other way to achieve these effects in 3D. It can be a tricky subject to get right because the movement and texture of smoke or fire is organic and changeable.

One way to accomplish these pyrotechnic effects is to substitute nonrenderable points in the particle system for spheres, which can then be textured to look like fire or smoke. By using a Fresnel shader in the Transparency channel of the material, the edges of the spheres dissolve to nothing, hiding the fact that geometry is being used. This can work well for fire and certain kinds of smoke.

If you want truly realistic smoke plumes, you have to ditch geometry and turn to volumetric rendering techniques. Volumetric rendering calculates the cumulative effect of semitransparent materials such as smoke and fire by rendering them as a true 3D volume. Whereas a texture map is really just a 2D image, curved and distorted on a 3D surface, a volumetric texture exists in all three dimensions. Rendering such effects can be time-consuming, but the results are worthwhile.

ADVANCED MODELING—EDGES

When modeling practically any rigid (nonorganic) object, it is crucial that you model edges correctly. This is something that most beginners in 3D overlook, because it's not obvious at first. But if you wonder why your 3D work just doesn't seem to look truly professional, this could be the reason.

If you look around your room or office, you'll see many real objects that have corners and edges. A table has a flat top with perpendicular sides that meet at 90°, and a CD case likewise. To take a slightly more complex example, look at the end of a ballpoint pen, with a domed cap stoppering a hexagonal shaft—all have edges.

You may be able to visualize simple 3D shapes that can easily represent these objects: a cube for the table top, an extruded profile for the CD case, or a cropped sphere and a cylinder for the pen. The problem is that in our quest to break down the real objects mentally into essential forms, it's too easy to oversimplify them, and the edges are often the first things to go.

Left: Here's the end of a pen, modeled using our deconstruction technique. All the parts are basically correct but the object looks fake. The reason is that all the edges are too sharp. In fact, the edges are perfect—something that never happens in reality.

Below: Here's the same object modeled more accurately. First we create a hexagon spline, then we round off the edges by chamfering the points.

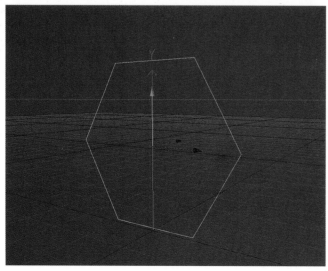

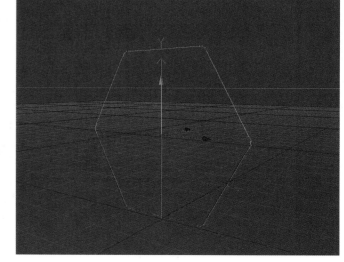

Below: These are lofted together with some circles to create the shaft of the pen. The end of a ballpoint pen has a nonhexagonal section, re-created here. The chamfered hexagons produce a softer, rounded edge to the edges of the pen, reflecting the original.

Bottom left: The cap of the loft is rounded. In the program we're using here, Cinema 4D, the rounding can be achieved parametrically; it's built into the Loft feature, so we just need to enable it and set the radius and subdivision. Already the object looks more solid and realistic.

Below: The cap is made not with a sphere but a lathe. The profile of the cap is not domed, it's angled—again, chamfering of the vertices helps to prevent any perfectly hard edges. Note that the underside is also chamfered so that the cap does not intersect the top of the shaft. The intersection would be another perfect edge.

Bottom right: The pen is rerendered in the same scene, and the results are remarkably better. Using an ordinary object like this is a good way to demonstrate the effect of edge detail in an object, because there is nothing else in the scene to support the realism of the model.

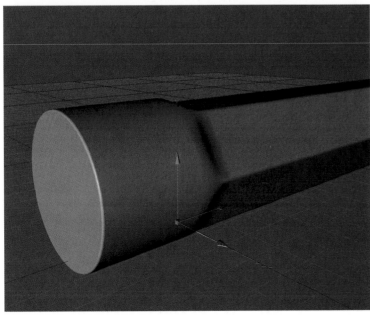

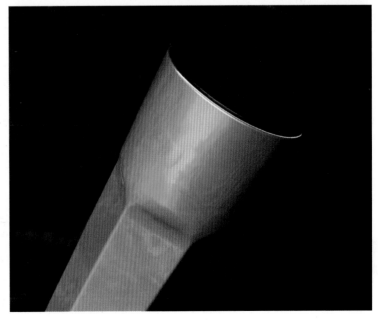

LOGO AND TYPE Type and logos are excellent subjects for 3D treatment and have been so since 3D began. The principle is extremely simple: take a logo, or some text, and extrude it to give it depth. This produces type that extends into the 3D dimension and can be treated like any other 3D object.

When creating 3D type there's one crucial thing to remember, and that's the edges of the text. When type is set in 2D on a page there's no problem with its readability (so long as the font is meant to be readable). We read text by recognizing the edges of the letters and the overall shape of the word, so black text on a white background is easy to read. Take text into a 3D program and extrude it and you complicate the edges of the text, especially if you choose a dramatic camera angle.

Radiant

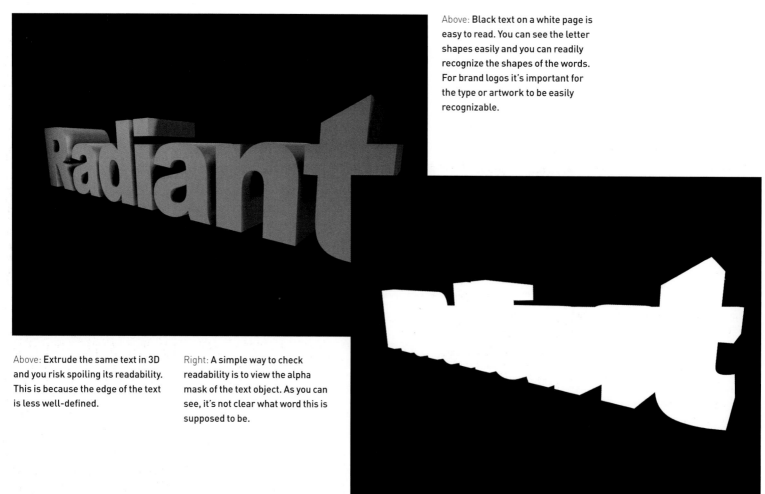

Above: Black text on a white page is easy to read. You can see the letter shapes easily and you can readily recognize the shapes of the words. For brand logos it's important for the type or artwork to be easily recognizable.

Above: **Extrude the same text in 3D and you risk spoiling its readability. This is because the edge of the text is less well-defined.**

Right: **A simple way to check readability is to view the alpha mask of the text object. As you can see, it's not clear what word this is supposed to be.**

Above left: **There are a few reasons why the 3D type is not reading well. There is not very much contrast between the front face of the type and the extruded side. This is partly to do with the lighting. A quick adjustment of the lighting increases the contrast between the sides and the face making the type a little easier to recognize.**

Above right: **It's still pretty confusing, so let's change the camera angle to make the type less distorted. Head-on and slightly from below keeps the type readable and also shows off the 3D-ness nicely. The depth of the type doesn't need to be overstated for it to look good in a still image.**

Right: **Another technique for improving the readability of 3D type is to have different colors for the face and sides of the type. Most 3D programs let you do this, although you can also do it manually by selecting the face polygons and creating a new object from them. As an alternative, you could use colored lights.**

LIGHTING AND ILLUMINATION
Lighting is crucial to any 3D scene, whether photorealistic or not. Lighting conveys mood and time of day and illuminates the form of objects in the scene. A poorly lit scene will never look convincing, no matter how great the animation, modeling, or texturing.

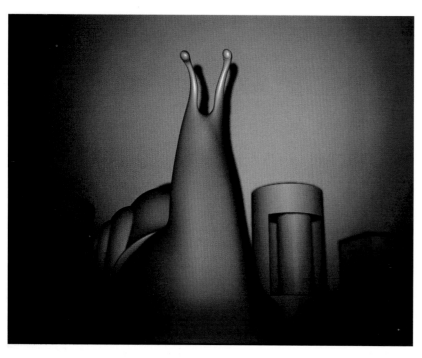

Lights have a few basic properties, and it will help to recognize and evaluate these independently of one another if you want to translate what you see in reality to the computer. These properties are intensity, color, spread, and direction. You can look at any photograph and evaluate the lighting using these terms.

To take a simple example, imagine a shot of a beach at high noon, midsummer on a cloudless day. Now think about the scene in terms of the properties above. Intensity: very high direct illumination from the sun results

Above left: **Here's a poor example of lighting. One spotlight illuminates the scene, and it's placed in line with the camera so that the light is head-on. This flattens out the renders, foreshortening the scene, and making object details difficult to see.**

Above right: **By moving the light up and to the side, we get much more spatial information in the scene. The Snail is brought forward in the image, and the depth of the scene is enhanced. But shadows are quite dark.**

in high contrast with bright highlights; the bright light also results in a high amount of bounced light which makes some shadow area less dense. Color: white with subtle blue ambient light from the skydome. Spread: with the sun, there is no attenuation of the light. Direction: depending on the location, from almost directly above.

Now imagine a street scene at night. It's raining. Intensity: very low, but with bright areas from artificial street lighting, and maybe some slight ambience from reflected light from low clouds and dark shadows. Color: A murky monotone orange. Spread: streetlights are strongly attenuated over distance and are throwing limited cones of light into the scene. Direction: straight down from the streetlights.

part 06. 3D techniques & design

Left: **A dim blue fill light on the opposite side of the scene fills in the shadow areas, providing some extra detail without washing the image out.**

Below left: **The previous two lights are reduced in intensity to about 10 per cent each and both aimed at the background objects only. The foreground subject is then illuminated with its own spotlight directly above. This not only picks out the subject more clearly but add a strong sense of isolation to the character in the scene.**

Above: **Another version of the same scene makes use of extra fill lighting on the snail and depth-of-field blurring for a more cinematic look and a forlorn feel for the central character.**

Left: **Lighting the background brightly and reducing the illumination of the subject turns the character into a silhouette. The result still focuses attention on the subject but in a more introverted, subtle way.**

NEGATIVE LIGHTS AND FALLOFF Lights in a 3D program can be set to cast negative illumination. This feature, available in most 3D programs, causes light not to be cast into the scene but to be sucked out of it. There is no real-world counterpart to this effect, of course, which is a useful byproduct of the 3D graphics systems.

Below: **Here are three spotlights with different falloff so you can see the effect. The left light has no falloff, the middle light has linear falloff, and the right light has inverse squared falloff. You can usually set different degrees of falloff, depending on the amount of attenuation required.**

3D lights can be set so that they decay naturally, preventing their illumination from spilling too far into the scene. This is a very useful feature, as it allows you some control over the lighting spread, helping to restrict it to where it is needed. Light falloff mimics the inverse-square law that governs the decay of light in the real world.

Opposite top left: **Falloff only goes so far. To mop up overspill from a light in specific places, you need negative lights. Take this example—one object casting a shadow over another. The green cylinder appears to be floating because there's nothing tying it visually to the floor on which it rests; it's already in shadow and the ambient and fill lights also used in the scene do not cast shadows.**

Opposite top right: **A negative light with a short falloff is placed under the cylinder to darken the floor under it to make it look as if there's some subtle ambient shadowing as if rendering using radiosity.**

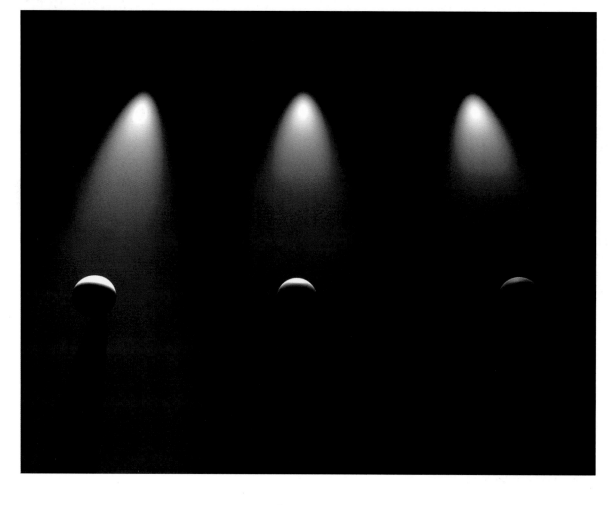

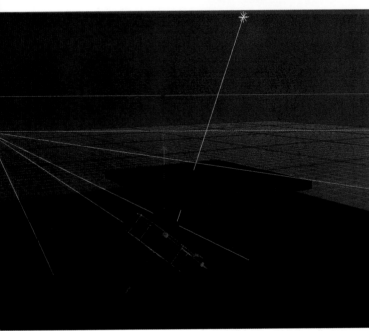

Above: Here's the scene in shaded view in Cinema 4D. You can see the three positive lights used in the scene (parallel, point fill, and ambient) plus the negative light at the base of the cylinder. In Cinema 4D, unlike some other apps, there is a special parallel spotlight that gives a disklike shadow. A very short falloff distance is used, along with a low brightness.

Above: Negative lights can also be used for special effects. Whereas positive lights cast dark shadows, negative lights cast bright ones. In this example, two shadow-casting point lights, one positive and one negative, and a blur fill, illuminate the subject. The positive light casts a normal dark shadow but the negative light is casting a light shadow. Uses of negative lights aren't always obvious, but it can be helpful to experiment with these effects, especially in illustration and creative design.

MATERIALS AND SURFACES The ability to simulate an object accurately in 3D has a lot to do with the surface quality of the object when it is rendered. Texture maps, material settings, and procedural shaders all combine to create a believable representation of a real or imagined object.

Designing surfaces is an art in itself, but one that can be mastered with practice and perseverance. Just as with modeling or lighting, you need to break down an object's appearance into components to evaluate and then replicate it in 3D. With 3D surfaces it's that much easier because a 3D program's material system is usually structured in a compartmentalized way. In reality most of the surface properties of an object are the result of a single phenomena—the reflection of light off its surface—but a 3D program breaks them down into specific components: diffuse, specular, ambient (more correctly luminosity), reflection, transparency, and bump. Some 3D programs have even more components, such as translucence, or split the components mentioned above into further subcomponents (such as diffuse into color and diffusion).

Ambient   Reflection   Bump   Specular   Diffuse

Above: **Here's a real object that displays most of the typical surface components.** Specular highlights are really reflections, and you can just make out some detail here of a window (the highlight is slightly square). Diffuse is the general illumination of the object surface, brightest facing the light and dimmer in areas not in direct line of sight of the main light source.

Ambient/Luminosity is the darkest part of the surface, and in this case it's very dark because, like most objects, the vase isn't self-illuminating. Glowing objects would have a high Ambient/Luminosity setting. The bump property shows all over the surface in various dimples, nicks, and scratches.

Right: Here's the 3D version of the same object. We've used several texture maps created in Photoshop, as well as a digital photo for the flower fabric, to re-create the object. The scene is rendered using radiosity so that the lighting matches the photo reference a little better. It's by no means perfect—a quick sketch rather than the finished work— but it shows you how much detail is required for even a simple surface like this vase.

Below: This is the diffuse/color texture used on the vase. It's loaded into the Color channel in Cinema 4D but it controls both the diffuse brightness and the color.

Below left: The bump map is also created in Photoshop. It has some large-scale clumping, which is quite low in contrast. This helps to create large-scale undulations in the surface. Finer "blips" create depressions in the surface, and these are darker and more intense because we want their bumps to be stronger.

Below: Reflection is enabled and a Fresnel shader is applied to attenuate the reflection on those parts of the surface that will be viewed head-on.

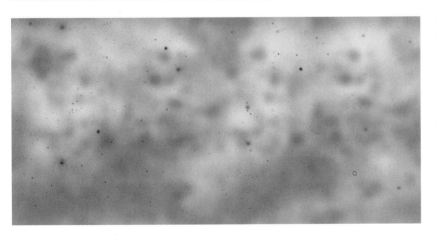

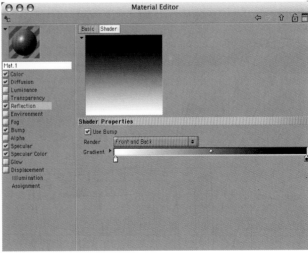

SPECIAL RENDERING TECHNIQUES—MULTIPASS

Multipass rendering is a special technique used to speed the iterative process of refining a 3D-rendered image. Traditionally if you needed to make a change to a scene, such as reducing or increasing the reflections on an object or making the shadows blacker, you had to rerender the whole scene again. With multipass rendering many of these changes can be done in a 2D compositing program such as Photoshop or After Effects.

How is this accomplished? Well, rather than rendering out a single flattened image file, the 3D application saves each of the components it renders to individual image files, either as separate files or as a layered Photoshop document. The latter makes it all the more easier to open and edit in a 2D app. Since internally the renderer calculates these buffers independently anyway, saving such a multilayered image doesn't significantly increase the rendering time.

The kinds of buffers that can be rendered varies between 3D programs but they usually include all the material channels such as Diffuse, Color, Specular, Reflections,

Below: **Here's a scene rendered using three lights and raytraced reflections as it comes out of the 3D program. This is a single image so editing it in a 2D program is relatively restrictive. You can change the overall brightness and contrast but not specific components.**

Luminosity, etc., plus shadows and any special-effect buffers, such as volumetric light glows or other post-effects. When you recombine the layers in Photoshop, the image looks as it would if it were rendered normally, except you have each of the component buffers on its own layer. If you need to boost the highlights, you can apply Levels to the Specular layer (or duplicate the layer in Screen mode) to make them brighter. The same goes for reflections or shadows or any other layers. For print work, when images are very large, this makes color correction and final tweaking of the image much easier. The same goes for animations, since the multipass rendering trick works the same here, too.

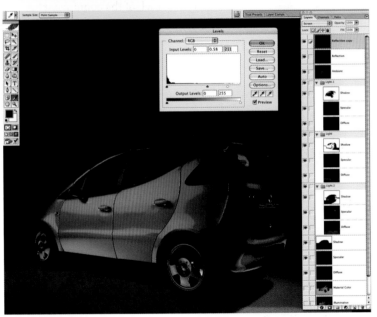

Top: The same scene—this time rendered using the multipass technique and opened in Photoshop. Each layer contains a specific part of the image, making it easy to make adjustments.

Above: Here we've made the reflections stronger by duplicating the reflection layer. Most of the layers are being combined using Screen mode in Photoshop, so that duplicating the layer doubles the intensity of the layer. Using Levels on the duplicate makes the reflections even brighter. Conversely, we could dim the reflections using Levels.

Top: The Multipass document has three layer folders—one for each light in the scene. Each folder contains the Diffuse, Specular and Shadow components that the light contributes to the scene. If we want to reduce the brightness of one of the lights, all we need to do is lower the Opacity of its Layer folder. That's much, much easier than rerendering the whole scene.

Above: You can easily add special effects, too. In this example the key light's Specular layer is duplicated, blurred, and then intensified using Levels. This creates a bloom effect on the specular highlights.

EXPORT AND OUTPUT—2D AND 3D FORMATS If you work in one 3D program and never leave it, or you never use files from any other source, importing and exporting files is of no concern to you. However, most professional 3D artists find they need to import foreign model formats into their chosen 3D program, or export a model or image for someone else who doesn't use the same software.

Since all 3D programs use their own proprietary file formats, you can't simply send them your current scene file (unless their 3D program supports it for import). More often than not an intermediary file format, supported by both 3D programs, can be used to exchange data. Welcome to the crazy world of 3D file exchange.

In the past, three file formats have become standards for transferring 3D models between 3D programs, with varying degrees of success. These are 3ds (the old 3D Studio file format), OBJ (Wavefront's native file format), and DXF (the file format native to AutoCAD). Almost all 3D programs support these three file formats, and most support the Lightwave LWO format too. However each format is implemented slightly differently in the 3D programs, meaning that transferring a mesh from 3ds max into ElectricImage using 3ds format, or moving a model from Maya to Cinema 4D using OBJ might not always work as smoothly as you might hope.

The thing that usually goes wrong is the scale. Importing a model from a foreign 3D program using a non-native file format often results in a model that might be tens, hundreds, or even thousands of times too big or too small for the scene you're planning to use it in. There is an easy fix: simply scale the object until it's the right size and then freeze the transformation (to reset the scale values to zero). Sometimes, though, the mesh itself can be damaged in the process of translating the file. A common problem is missing or damaged Normals, which can make the surface appear inside out or malformed. Again most software can fix this, but sometimes you have to re-export the model using a different format or settings.

Textures can be exported with models but you have to have UV mapping saved in the model file—proprietary mapping modes will not transfer, meaning you would have to retexture the model in the destination program.

Top: **FBX supports volumetric effect such as smoke and fire as seen in this scene. The dancing fireman utilizes motion-capture data, too.**

Above: **FXB files support standard keyframe animation and IK. This running, fire-breathing, smoke-blowing TRex has smoothly deforming skin as it runs in real-time in Quicktime player.**

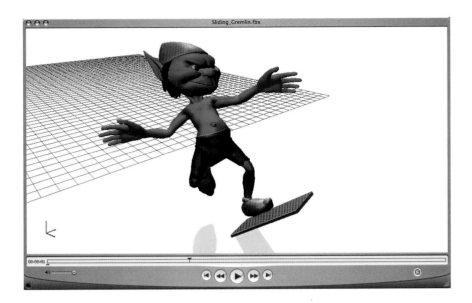

Left: **FBX** will likely be the future standard for transferring complex 3D scene data between different 3D applications. **FBX** for Quicktime lets you view complex 3D scenes inside Apple's standard media viewer. You can view the scene fully shaded and textured or as a wireframe, shaded or flat-filled, and navigate the view just as in a 3D program.

This is just model and texture data. If you want to transfer an animation as well (for instance, so it can be rendered using a better or faster renderer), forget it. This is just too complicated a process to work. There have been attempts at translating animation from app to app but most result in a lot of clean up work.

However all this will hopefully be ancient history thanks to a company called Kaydara and its 3D file format called FBX. FBX, if supported by all the major 3D companies, looks to be the panacea for 3D file transfers. With FBX you can move models, animation, and skeleton hierarchies between 3D programs seamlessly, so the theory goes, and by and large FBX seems to be delivering the goods. FBX supports both NURBS and polygons, morph targets and shape animation, keyframes and motion-capture data, IK, lights, cameras, and textures, too.

FBX is so well designed that Apple and Kaydara have even implemented FBX import capability to Apple's Quicktime media player. This lets you load and view 3D animations saved into FBX format from any 3D program. The player renders the scene in real time using OpenGL just as if it were in the native 3D program and it's quite stunning to watch. You can export movie files from the Quicktime player, share animations, and let colleagues or clients view your work, etc.

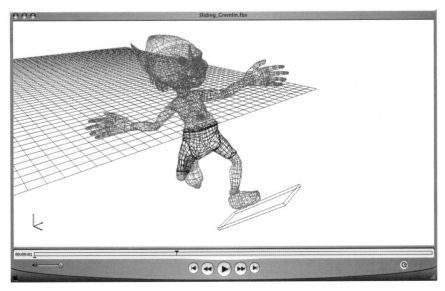

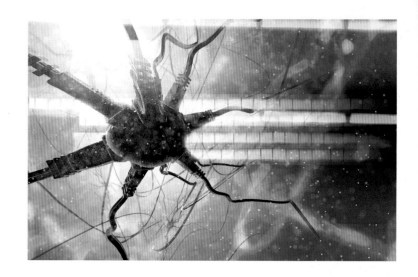

PART 06. 3D TECHNIQUES & DESIGN

CHAPTER TWO

3D DESIGN IN ACTION

After the last few chapters 3D design might sound like a science, but remember that it also should be an art. Like any art you need a grasp of the theory to get beyond a basic level, but the theory makes a lot more sense when you see it in practice. Professional designers accumulate tricks and shortcuts as they go, searching for new ways to create particular effects, and often sharing them with the 3D community at large. With experience, careful observation, and some lateral thinking, complex rendering techniques can be faked and more realistic results can be achieved.

The examples in this chapter show some of these methods in action, detailing the thinking behind them and the techniques being used. The following gallery section showcases stunning work from some of the best 3D minds in the business. Throughout, one thing should become clear: modeling, lighting, and rendering by the book can get you so far, but only imagination and experimentation will help you develop a unique visual style of your own.

NEURONS The idea for this magazine illustration was based on the concept of "plug-ins" for 3D applications, and the subject was illustrated by creating neurons that looked like electrical plugs and outlets. The look of the illustration was to be quite detailed and organic and there were several visual tricks used to suggest a photographed organic environment, including depth of field and lens distortion. In order to complete such an illustration to the tight deadlines, it was clear that most of the "scene" would be constructed in Photoshop, with the 3D program rendering out elements as and when they were needed. This allowed for experimentation with the composition of the final image since individual rendered elements were on their own layers and could be repositioned easily.

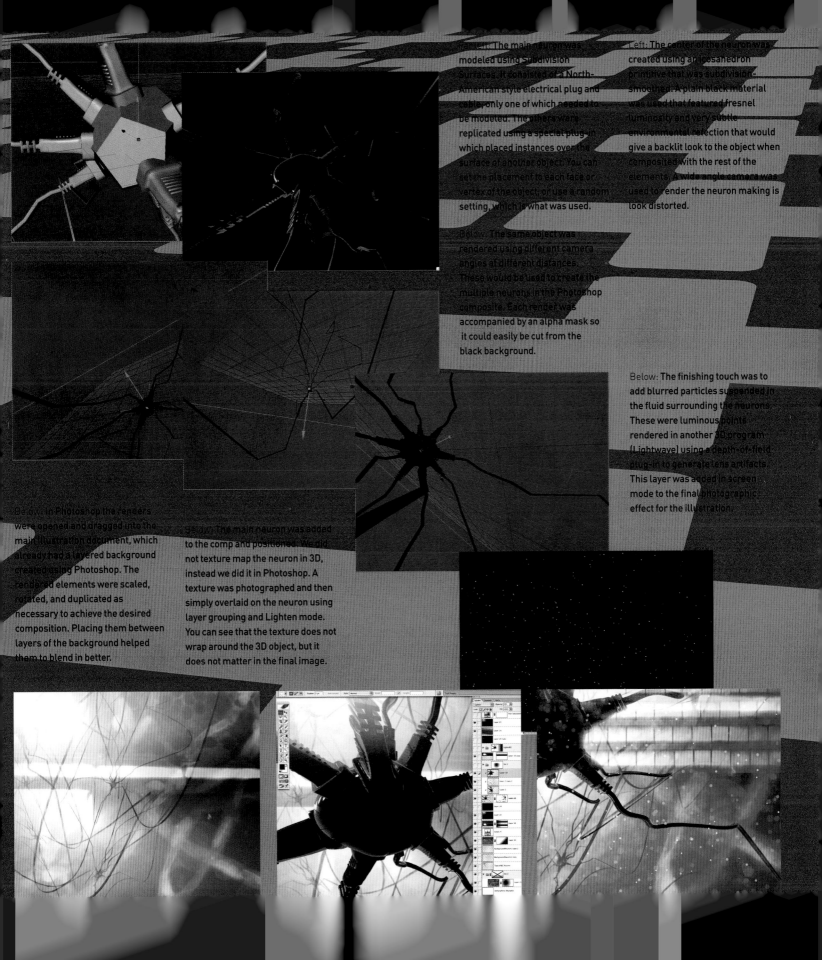

Far left: The main neuron was modeled using Subdivision Surfaces. It consisted of a North-American style electrical plug and cable, only one of which needed to be modeled. The others were replicated using a special plug-in which placed instances over the surface of another object. You can set the placement to each face or vertex of the object, or use a random setting, which is what was used.

Below: The same object was rendered using different camera angles at different distances. These would be used to create the multiple neurons in the Photoshop composite. Each render was accompanied by an alpha mask so it could easily be cut from the black background.

Left: The center of the neuron was created using an icosahedron primitive that was subdivision-smoothed. A plain black material was used that featured fresnel luminosity and very subtle environmental reflection that would give a backlit look to the object when composited with the rest of the elements. A wide angle camera was used to render the neuron making is look distorted.

Below: The finishing touch was to add blurred particles suspended in the fluid surrounding the neurons. These were luminous points rendered in another 3D program (Lightwave) using a depth-of-field plug-in to generate lens artifacts. This layer was added in screen mode to the final photographic effect for the illustration.

Below: In Photoshop the renders were opened and dragged into the main illustration document, which already had a layered background created using Photoshop. The rendered elements were scaled, rotated, and duplicated as necessary to achieve the desired composition. Placing them between layers of the background helped them to blend in better.

Below: The main neuron was added to the comp and positioned. We did not texture map the neuron in 3D, instead we did it in Photoshop. A texture was photographed and then simply overlaid on the neuron using layer grouping and Lighten mode. You can see that the texture does not wrap around the 3D object, but it does not matter in the final image.

EXPLODING HEAD Modern digital illustrations frequently merge multiple design disciplines and media. The inclusion of 3D elements in an illustration or the heavy manipulation of 3D renders in Photoshop are common practices that can yield some interesting results. In this image a series of figurative 3D renders have been composited together with abstract "3d junk" and stock photography to create a dynamic, explosive image. This image was produced for *Digit* magazine in the UK using Maxon's Cinema 4D and Adobe Photoshop.

The main model was created in Cinema 4D using one of the stock human figures. This was modeled in several stages to add extra detail. An explosion deformer added to the model explodes the polygons to create the chaotic base underpinning the image. This was rendered using a combination of normal and wireframe rendering, which further enhances the detail and complexity.

Left: Filters are then applied to remove most of the hard CG look and impart a photographic quality to the render. These include a depth-of-field blurring and photographic black-and-white film filtering. The original render would still later be used, overlaid, and applied using various blending modes.

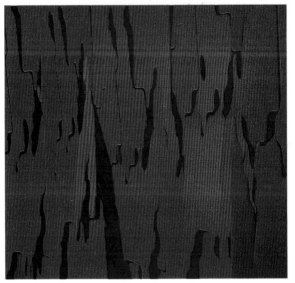

Left: This is an example of how a seemingly nonsense 3D object can be converted in Photoshop more usefully as an abstract shape layer. It can often be quicker to experiment in this way than search through photo CDs for just the right image.

Left: The meat of this image comes together in Photoshop by blending in various abstract shapes, images, and textures over the rendered 3D objects. The fractured face is actually created by hand in Photoshop from a render of the unexploded head object. Sections are cut out, transformed, and the edges painted in by hand.

The result is an image that blends 2D and 3D in seamless fashion. Even in the workflow used there is little distinction made between 2D and 3D processes. Modern digital illustrators are free to move between various applications in the construction of a digital composite image.

STORMY SEASCAPE Creating large bodies of water is a challenge for a 3D artist. Water is dynamic, it changes and moves, it reacts to light in surprising ways, and can look very different depending on the kind of water it is. In this illustration the aim was to create a realistic ocean complete with froth and waves. The first step in producing an image such as this is to do some research. Photographic images of stormy seas were gathered and various qualities were noted.

The first thing that became apparent was that in a storm, where dark clouds reduce visibility, the water looks neither transparent nor particularly reflective. In fact it looks opaque, and usually dark gray-blue rather than bright blue. Water itself is actually blue, but the blueness of the sea's surface comes from the reflection of the sky. With no bright blue sky to reflect the water looks dark and foreboding.

Right: The sea is created from a single, flat subdivision surface plane. The plane is heavily subdivided during rendering to create a finer end result when displaced and viewed up close.

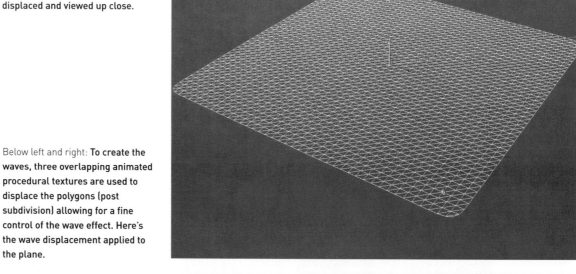

Below left and right: To create the waves, three overlapping animated procedural textures are used to displace the polygons (post subdivision) allowing for a fine control of the wave effect. Here's the wave displacement applied to the plane.

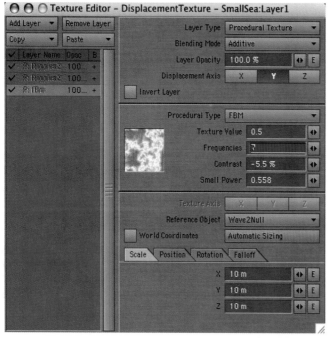

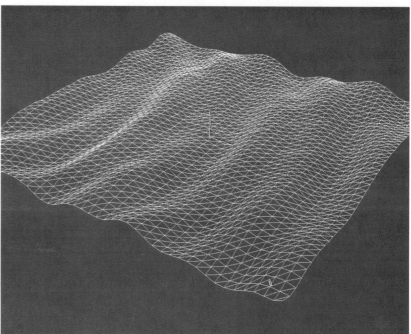

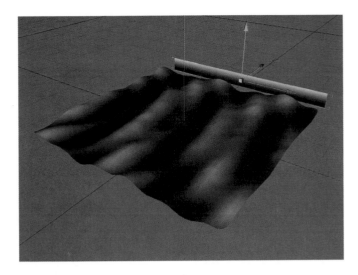

Above: **Texturing the water surface is tricky, but the animated waves actually help the process. The churning waters of a wave crest tend to look whiter than the rest of the sea surface. Using a simple** black-and-white gradient applied through the plane using flat (planar) mapping automatically makes wave crests lighter, and this texture is applied in the wave material's luminosity channel.

Above: **The rest of the texturing involves various fractal shaders in the bump, diffuse, and luminosity channels, along with a small amount of Fresnel reflection, but no transparency at all. Scene fog and a background sky image complete the scene. Lightwave's "crumple" shader was used extensively as it provides an excellent wavelet shader.**

Below: **When animated. the waves roll slowly helping to indicate their scale, and they become whiter as they get higher.**

chapter 02. 3D design in action

BIKE 3D graphics offers a great deal of creative opportunity for those who like to experiment. The illustration featured here is a case in point. The premise was to create an abstract illustration using relatively flat colors. Sections of 3D objects would serve as component parts of the illustration. The main elements of the artwork would be composition, form, color, and detail. The technique amounted to digital collage, but achieved using an unusual route.

3D programs usually employ something called clipping planes. These are distance limits imposed on the 3D camera so that objects too close to the camera or very far away do not cause serious rendering problems and slowdowns. Near clipping planes are more common than far ones, and all 3D programs have them. Usually you don't notice the effect of clipping planes unless you reduce the scale of an object by a large amount and attempt to move the camera in close to make the object fill the frame once more. This usually occurs when importing an object from a different 3D program or the Web, where scale disparities are common. The solution is simply to scale the object back up to the right size suitable for your 3D program.

However clipping planes offer you the ability to create slices through an object, like practical model cutaways. For the purpose of this illustration, clipping planes provided a quick way to create complex abstract shapes for the collage.

Above: **Clipping planes are usually not meant to be seen directly, but they can let you create object cutaways without resorting to Boolean modeling procedures. For the illustration a bike model was used as the source.**

Opposite, top 4 images: **The bike was scaled down and the 3D camera was zoomed toward it until clipping occurred. Then the view was rotated to orbit the bike and therefore clip it at different angles. Once a relatively interesting shape was generated, it was rendered at high resolution. Textures are removed to give a plain gray surface revealing the geometry more clearly. Because there is no raytracing involved at all, the images are rendered very quickly even at high resolution.**

Opposite, bottom: **Each render is then opened in Photoshop and composited together to create the 3D collage. Copying and transforming the layers gives the impression that more than 4 renders have been used, so the result is fairly complex. Color is introduced into the grayscale renders using standard Photoshop techniques, including Hue/Saturation adjustment, layer styles, and blend modes.**

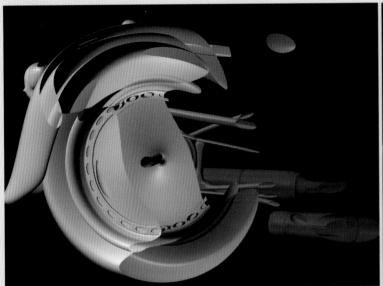

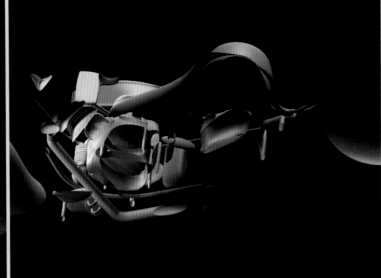

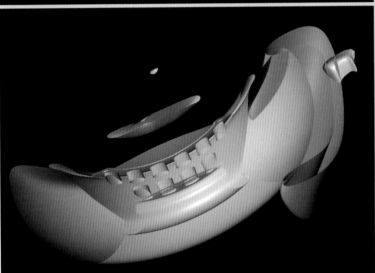

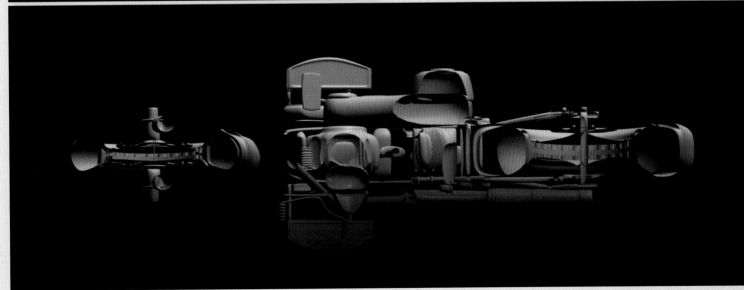

3D AND 2D COMPOSITES While entire scenes can be created in a 3D program, it is often required that 3D rendered elements be composited with live footage. This is typically done in movie special effects, television, and advertising where a real background image or footage is combined with 3D elements seamlessly.

This image is an example of combining 3D-rendered object with a background image. It may seem a trivial task, but it's one of the most difficult to get right. The key to a great composite image is the lighting, and there are numerous ways in which to get it spot on.

In this example a technique was used where the different scene lighting components are rendered separately and then recombined in Photoshop. This lets you control the intensity of the different lights without having to rerender each time you make a change.

There are three main lighting components rendered: Diffuse (and specular), ambient, and a special "bounce" light. The latter is used to simulate the greenish light bouncing up from the ground, illuminating the underside of the planes.

Right: Here are the lighting passes used for this scene. This is the diffuse pass for the key light—in this case, the sun. The direction of the light is matched to the background image by looking at the shadows cast by objects in the photo.

Far right: The ambient pass simulates the blue diffused light from the sky that tints areas that are in shadow.

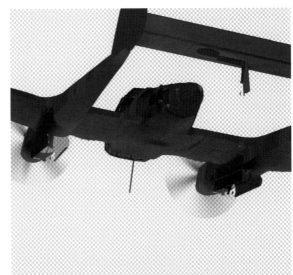

Right: The bounce light is a special upward-facing directional light tinted a green color. This is sunlight reflected back upward by the foliage in the photograph.

Far right: It's important to note that the strength of each light is set to 100% in the 3D program. No attempt is made here to match the scene lighting. Therefore if all three layers are composited at full opacity, the result does not look convincing.

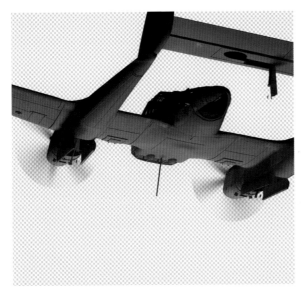

Right: However by adjusting how much each layer contributes to the composite, the lighting can be adjusted to match the photography very closely. There's still one more trick to perform though.

Far right: Notice that the distant hill is much bluer than the foreground. This is due to absorption of the light by haze in the air. A flat blur layer in Photoshop can be added using a layer mask to attenuate the amount of blue applied to each plane; the most distant one having the most blue.

SPIDER This architectural object is made from a combination of Subdivision Surfaces and deformed primitives, and makes use of HDRI environment maps to provide the surface reflections. HDRI is a technique that has gained prominence in 3D over the years. Though it's primarily used to generate scene illumination when combined with radiosity rendering, it can also be used to produce realistic specular and environment reflections.

Because specular highlights are really just reflections, HDR images with their huge dynamic range can be used to create realistic highlights on reflective objects as an alternative to using the normal material specular channel.

Below: The pads which clamp the glass are created using round-edged cylinders. These are flared outward using a bulge deformer. They could have been made by lathing a curve but a deformed primitive offers more flexibility, as the resolution and rounding of its edges remain "live" even while deformed. This makes it easier to make changes later if needed.

Right: The object begins life as a Subdivision Surface model. Using a simple cube as a starting point, four polygon faces are extruded out and edited to make the curved arms of the object.

Below: Once modeled, the object's materials are defined. The chrome material is a special shader that uses both raytraced reflections and an environment reflection map. The shader is set up so that the environment maps is occluded by objects in the scene (i.e., the scene reflections and the environment map are not summed where they overlap). This lets you use both together.

Below far right: The Environment map is an HDR image downloaded from www.debevec.org. Its intensity is reduced so that it does not wash out the surface and only the brightest parts are reflected.

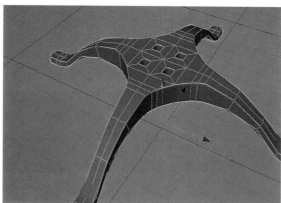

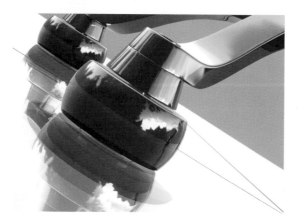

SIMULATING RADIOSITY AND GI Before Radiosity and Global illumination rendering became a practical alternative rendering technique, creating photorealistic images with accurate lighting involved faking the effects of bounced lighting in a scene. Despite the speed of modern computers making radiosity much more viable, the ability to fake this look is still a skill in demand. One of the reasons for this is that animation is still quite difficult to do using radiosity, due to the noise that radiosity-rendered images tend to have. The noise is not offensive in a still image—in fact it often adds to the effect—but in an animation it can cause shimmering and is very distracting. Even for still images, a 3D artist may choose not to render using radiosity because they may need more control over the lighting than radiosity rendering allows.

Top: The illustration is a still image rendered using techniques that mimic the effect of bounced lighting. The scene is indoors lit by a single bright light source, suggesting an open window. However rendering the scene with a single light does not result in a realistic image.

Above: In reality the light striking the floor, walls, and pots would bounce around the room until completely absorbed. The result of this is that areas not directly illuminated by the initial rays are not totally black but have some subtle illumination. Adding a front-facing distant light set to a low value adds some secondary illumination to the wall and pots.

Top: Two further distant lights angled inward slightly and placed behind the wall are added. Light exclusion is used to prevent them from illuminating or being blocked by the wall. This adds a secondary bounce from the wall to the backs of the pots. It's not 100 per cent accurate and some artistic license is involved; the lights also serve to illuminate the edges of the pots for a rim-light effect, which helps them stand out from the background.

Above: A final spotlight is added just to even out the illumination. Note that no ambient light is used at all, just carefully placed lights. The final touch is adding a bloom effect on the glazed vases at the front. This is done using a Lightwave plug-in, called (not surprisingly) "bloom."

AE1 Accurately modeling an object involves paying close attention to the finer details. This scene is a good example. While it might sound strange, a complex object doesn't actually need so much fine detail. It will take longer to model, of course, but the complexity means that it will have visual interest built in. A simple model doesn't have that advantage, so to prevent it from looking computer-generated it has to be very well made.

This hi-fi loudspeaker begins life as a box. A simple cube primitive is used, then this is scaled to the correct proportions, and—importantly—its edges are rounded to the correct radius. Even if the object has sharp edges you should still round them—the most tiny rounding radius can still make a big difference. In fact, there are many very small details in this model that have a dramatic impact on the final image. You might not notice them at first, but you would definitely do so if they were absent.

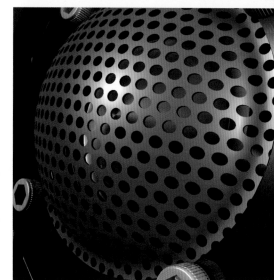

Far left: **Notice the difference between these three boxes. The right two have rounding, while the left one does not. Although the middle box has a minute rounding radius it's enough to give its edge a little thickness. It catches the light and makes the object appear more solid. Rounding is applied wherever possible on the model.**

Above left: **The object is finely polished, but it does have a subtle woodgrain texture in the Bump channel. Carefully adjusting the bump level is crucial, or it will look like the surface is too rough. Note that the bump is only just visible here in the specular highlight.**

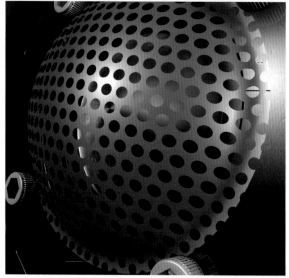

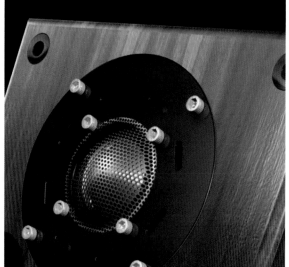

Left: **The grille over the tweeter is created using a clip map. The downside, however, is that the object has no thickness, which is a shortfall of using clipping maps in this way. However, this is not a problem. We can make a duplicate of the grille object, move it backward a fraction, and give its material a dark color with no reflection or highlights. The trick makes it look as if the grille has a thickness, but it's really just the result of the offset object.**

This page: **Close inspection of the materials used in the real object lets you duplicate their qualities in 3D. The bass driver is made from a spun aluminum. To achieve this an anisotropic specular shader was used to produce the elongated highlights and radial scratches. The foam suspension uses an Oren Nayer shader, which gives a more matte look than a normal Phong shader could manage. Noise provides the bump for the foam, and it's given a slight touch of color rather than being flat gray.**

06.03
3D GALLERY

Below: **The 3D work of Kyoshi Harada is astonishingly detailed. This image, Zero Fighter, features a model so detailed that you can see each nut and rivet. Kyoshi traced a drawing with Adobe Illustrator, then used the data as a template with the Japanese 3D** application "Shade." Due to Shade's slow rendering, Kyoshi imports the model as a DXF into Lightwave, making adjustments as necessary and applying surface definitions to the parts.

Kyoshi Harada
harada@cc22.ne.jp

part 06. 3D techniques and design

Below right: **Jeremy A. Engleman** is a master of composition and one of the few 3D artists to successfully create genuine art. His works combine low-resolution model "sketches" in tandem with precision lighting.
Jeremy A. Engleman
www.art.net/~jeremy/

Right: **Pavel Fedorchuk works as a 3D artist for a leading Russian software and games development provider, Nikita. In his spare time he works on his own 3D art using 3ds max, entering and often winning 3D competitions such as those run by 3Dluvr.com. The image featured here is a typical example of his work entered into the Mythical Creatures 3Dluvr contest, and showcases some great fur-rendering techniques.**
Pavel Fedorchuk
goldengrifon@mail.ru

3D GALLERY

Opposite: **Derek Lea**, a Canadian illustrator of considerable talent, is another artist who finds the marriage of 3D with illustration a good one. Derek details the technicalities of this illustration, "The hand mesh was rendered in Poser 3.0 as an animation frame. All 3D objects were created in Strata 3D pro. The little neutrino bug was a shape that was used as instances since there were so many of them. All finished renders were combined and manipulated in Photoshop."
Derek Lea
www.dereklea.com

Right: **3D is not an obvious tool for illustration work, yet the two are strangely harmonious.** Bill Ledger's comic images are populated with bizarre figures that ooze character from every pixel. Working from sketches, the talented artist transforms the 2D ideas into 3D scenes, yet manages to lose nothing in translation, as these images testify.
Bill Ledger
www.billledger.com

Right: **Says Bill on his website, "I produce cartoon art for publishing, new media, advertising, and TV to clients all over the world. With new technologies my styles are progressive and adapting all the time."** Bill has been nominated for the D&AD packaging design and illustration award and has been featured on the cover of *Contact 18*, the source book for those looking for illustrators to hire.

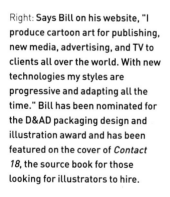

Left: **Creating realistic humans is one of the most difficult jobs in 3D. Creating them with believable character and photoreal surfacing and lighting is nearly impossible. The quality of Koji Yamagami's stunning 3D render almost defies belief. But it's no surprise. Using 3DS Max and Splutterfish's Brazil rendering plug-in, Koji routinely creates images like this for his company Beans Magic Co.**
Koji Yamagami
www.beans-magic.com/

Below: **The still life reinterpreted by the Valencian 3D artist Carles Piles. Piles models and textures in Maxon Cinema 4D, then applies an intensive spot-lighting regime to balance realism against his trademark painterly style. He then readjusts the shading for an optimal effect. "My goal is just one; to imagine something, obtain sufficient visual references for what I imagined, and then create it."**
Carles Piles
www.carlespiles.com

Below: **It's rare to find a 3D artist that can bend, mold, and soften 3D imagery into something much more organic and natural, and Francois Gutherz is one of the those rarities. Combining a 3D renderer with Photoshop is a good way to create less sterile-looking 3D work, of which Francois is a prime exponent.**
Francois Gutherz
www.fra.planet-d.net

3D GALLERY

Right: **There are few 3D artists whose work is so immediately recognizable (or disturbing) as Meats Meier. While currently employed at The Orphanage, a special-effects house in San Francisco, Meats still finds time to create personal works of art and work on freelance projects. "My goal is to one day be the first person to complete a full-length 3D movie completely on my own. To reach this goal I have spent the last seven years studying every needed skill—modeling, texturing, rigging, animation, lighting, rendering, and everything from compositing to sound editing."**

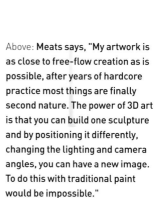

Above: **Meats says, "My artwork is as close to free-flow creation as is possible, after years of hardcore practice most things are finally second nature. The power of 3D art is that you can build one sculpture and by positioning it differently, changing the lighting and camera angles, you can have a new image. To do this with traditional paint would be impossible."**

Opposite: **"With 3D," Meats adds, "the possibilities are 'virtually' endless. I usually end up with at least 200 images before I get bored with a concept. I enjoy looking back and being able to see what led up to what I would call a final image. Also, I can see other paths that I could have chosen along the way, which usually leads to the next concept..."**
Meats Meier
www.3dartspace.com

3D GALLERY

Left: Architectural 3D artist Chen Qingfeng's work combines great modeling with even better lighting and rendering, an essential skill for architectural 3D work. Chen's images are rendered using radiosity techniques with Autodesk's Lightscape.
Chen Qingfeng
cqfcqf.digitalart.org

Left: Moving and modeling one head and four limbs is hard enough, but Daniel Phillips pushes the boundaries by creating a character with three heads and six limbs on a single torso. We can only imagine how tricky it would be to rig and animate this monstrous character.
Daniel Phillips
http://dcp.lihp.com

Right: Peder Aversten's 3D work is humorous, quirky, and cool. This image was created by building 3D models in Maya and then overlaying them with still images in Photoshop. "Art is a way of living for me. I do fine-art, sculpture, digital art, 3D, and video production. You could almost classify it as multimedia because I like to experiment a lot."
Peder Aversten
aversten@meshmen.com

Above: **Combine intense model making with photoreal surfacing, lighting, and rendering and you get the wonderful work of Reinhard Claus. The details in this teapot model have been constructed with an intense eye for detail, and this goes double for the surface material. An HDRI environment adds the necessary reflections and highlights in this excellent render.**
Reinhard Claus
rc@claus-figuren.de

Right: **US-born, Berlin-based David Maas produced this 3D illustration for German power company EAM. David is an illustrator and 3D artist using Lightwave, and says of the image he created, "In the original street poster, one penguin is showing off his new pad and bragging about the cheap cooling costs: 'it wasn't cheap but the living costs are a joke.' It was so popular that the agency commissioned an encore: these two blokes ended up illustrating an entire brochure. The 3D approach made it economical, as the same figures and objects could be reused in new poses."**
David Maas
www.stickman.de

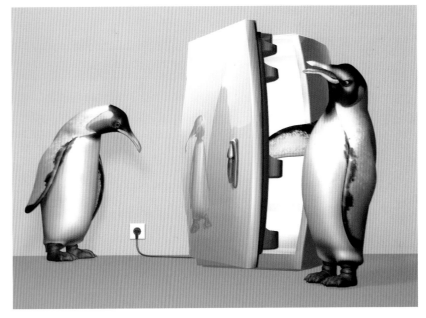

REFERENCE

07

GLOSSARY

Aliasing The jagged edge of bitmapped images or fonts occurring either when aliasing resolution is insufficient or when the images have been enlarged. This is caused by the pixels—which are square with straight sides—making up the image becoming visible. Sometimes called "jaggies", "staircasing", or "stairstepping."

Alpha channel A place where information regarding the transparency of a pixel is kept. In image files this is a separate channel—additional to the three RGB channels—where "masks" are stored.

Ambient A term used in 3D modeling software to describe a light source with no focus or direction, such as that which results from bouncing off all objects in a scene.

Antialiasing A technique of optically eliminating the jagged effect of bitmapped images or text reproduced on low-resolution devices such as monitors. This is achieved by blending the color at the edges of the object with its background by averaging the density of the range of pixels involved. Antialiasing is also employed to filter texture maps, such as those used in 3D applications, to eliminate signs of pixelation.

API (Application Programming Interface) A layer of code, built in or added to a computer operating system, which creates a bridge between an application (e.g. a 3D package) and computer hardware (e.g. a 3D graphics card). As long as both the software and the hardware support the same API, neither needs to be configured to support the other, enabling many applications to run on many different types of hardware without any need for recoding.

Area light A special light type that emits from a 2D area rather than a single point.

Axis An imaginary line that defines the centre of the 3D universe. In turn, the x, y, and z axes (width, height, and depth, respectively) define each of the three dimensions of an object. The axis along which an object rotates is the axis of rotation.

B-Spline A type of curve, similar to a Bezier curve but based on more complex formulae. B-Splines have additional control points and values, allowing a higher degree of control over a more localized area.

Bevel To round or chamfer an edge. Can also mean to extrude a polygon along its Normal, producing bevels around its perimeter.

Bézier spline In 3D and drawing applications, a curved line between two "control" points. Each point is a tiny database, or "vector", storing data about the line, such as its thickness, color, length, and direction. Complex shapes can be applied to the curve by manipulating "handles", which are dragged out from the control points.

Blend The merging of two or more colors, forming a gradual transition from one to the other.

Boolean Named after G. Boole, a 19th-century English mathematician, Boolean is used to describe a shorthand for logical computer operations, such as those that link values ("and", "or", "not", "nor", etc., called "Boolean operators"). In 3D applications, these operations can be used to join two objects together or remove one shape from another.

Bounding Box A rectangular box, available in certain applications, which encloses an item so that it can be resized or moved. In 3D applications, the bounding box is parallel to the axes of the object.

Bump map A bitmap image file, normally grayscale, applied to a surface material. The gray values in the image are assigned height values, with black representing the troughs and white the peaks. When applied to a surface and rendered the surface takes on an impression of relief.

CAD (computer-aided design) Strictly speaking, any design carried out using a computer, but the term is generally used with reference to 3D design, such as product design or architecture, where a computer software application is used to construct and develop complex structures.

Camera A viewpoint in a 3D application, defined by position, angle and lens properties, used to generate a view of a scene during modeling or rendering. Cameras can also be moved during animation, in the same way a movie camera moves during a conventional shoot.

Cartesian coordinates The coordinate system employed in 3D applications, which uses numbers to locate points in 3D space in relation to a theoretical point of origin where the three dimensional axes intersect.

Channel A bitmap image or a set of parameters used to define a component of a texture material.

Clipping plane In 3D applications, a plane beyond which an object is not visible. Most 3D views have six clipping planes: top, bottom, left, right, front, and back.

Collision detection The ability of a 3D program to calculate the proximity of objects and prevent them from intersecting.

Concave polygon A polygon whose shape is concave, for example, a star shape.

Convex polygon A polygon whose shape is convex, for example, a regular hexagon shape.

Coordinates Numerical values that define locations in 2D or 3D space.

Diffuse A color texture map applied to a surface to define its colors when viewed in direct light, and how much of the light that hits that surface will be absorbed and how much will be reflected—i.e. how much of those colors we can see.

part 07. reference

Digital Anything operated by, or created from, information or signals represented by binary digits, such as a digital recording. As distinct from analog, in which information is represented by a physical variable (in a recording this may be via the grooves in a vinyl platter).

Displacement map A grayscale bitmap image which operates similarly to a bump map, but differs in that the black, white, and gray values will affect the geometry of the surface underneath. Displacement mapping creates a more realistic texture than bump mapping at the cost of additional time computing the effects.

Environment map A 2D image that is projected onto the surface of a 3D object to simulate an environmental reflection.

Extrapolate Creating new values for a parameter based on the values that have gone before.

Extrude The process of duplicating the cross section of a 2D object, placing it in a 3D space at a distance from the original and creating a surface that joins the two together. For example, when extruded, two circles become a tube.

Face In 3D modeling, one flat "side" of an object, e.g. one of six sides of a cube.

Fall-off In a 3D environment, the degree to which light or another parameter loses intensity away from its source.

Fillet A curved surface that is created between two adjoining or intersecting surfaces. Fillets turn up most frequently in NURBS modeling.

Forward Kinematics Traditional animation is based on Forward Kinematics, where, for example, to make a character reach for an object, first the upper arm is rotated, then the forearm and then the hand.

Frame An individual still image extracted from an animation sequence. The basic divisor of time in animation.

Fresnel An effect where the edge of an object brightens due to an increased intensity of reflection along the edge.

Function curve In an application, a user-definable curve used to control the speed or intensity of motion or an effect.

Geometry What 3D objects are made out of, or rather described by. Geometry types include polygons, NURBS, and Bézier patches.

Gimbal lock In 3D applications, a situation in which an object cannot be rotated around one or more axes.

Glow A material parameter used to create external glows on objects. The glow usually extends beyond the object surface by a defined amount.

Height map An image used to displace or deform geometry. See Displacement Map.

Hidden Surface Removal A rendering method, usually wireframe, that prevents surfaces that cannot be seen from the given view from being drawn.

Interpolation A computer calculation used to estimate unknown values that fall between known ones. One use of this process is to redefine pixels in bitmapped images after they have been modified in some way—for instance, when an image is resized (called "resampling") or rotated, or if color corrections have been made. In such cases the program makes estimates from the known values of other pixels lying in the same or similar ranges.

Inverse Kinematics Or IK for short. When animating hierarchical models, IK can be applied so that moving the lowest object in the hierarchy has an effect on all the objects further up. This is the inverse of how Forward Kinematics works.

Lathe In 3D applications, the technique of creating a 3D object by rotating a 2D profile around an axis—just like carving a piece of wood on a real lathe.

Layer Modern image-editing applications can separate elements of an image onto transparent layers, stacked on top of each other to form a composite image. By switching layers on and off, changing their order, or changing the way they interact with each other, a designer can rework the composite image in a vast number of ways.

Map An image applied to a texture channel of a material.

Material The aggregate of all surface attributes for an object.

Memory The recall of digital data on a computer. Typically, this refers to either "dynamic RAM", the volatile "random access" memory that is emptied when a computer is switched off (data need to be stored on media such as a hard disk for future renewal), or ROM, the stable "read only" memory that contains unchanging data, for example the basic startup and initialization functions of most computers.

Mesh Vertices Vertices that are linked together to form Polygon or NURBS (or other) surfaces.

Motion channel An animation parameter that controls how an object moves (for example, rotation x, y, z and translation x, y, z are all Motion channels).

Multi-pass rendering The process whereby a single scene is rendered in multiple passes, each pass producing an image (or movie or image sequence) containing a specific portion of the scene but not all of it (for example, one part of a multi-pass render may contain just the reflections in the scene, or just the specular highlights).

Normal In 3D objects, the direction that is perpendicular to the surface of the polygon to which it relates.

NURBS Non-Uniform Rational B-Spline. A B-spline curve or a mesh of B-spline curves used to

GLOSSARY

define a line or a surface in a 3D application. NURBs surfaces require fewer points than polygons to model smooth flowing surfaces.

Parallax The apparent movement of two objects relative to each other when viewed from different positions.

Phong shading A superior method of shading surfaces that computes the shading of every pixel by interpolating data from the surface normals.

Pixel Acronym of picture element. The smallest component of a digitally generated image, such as a single dot of light on a computer monitor.

Plug-in A small program that "plugs-in" to an application to extend its features or add support for a particular file format.

Polygon Any 2D shape with more than three sides. Polygons—usually triangles, but sometimes quads—are joined together in 3D applications to create the surfaces of 3D objects.

Primitive A basic geometric element (e.g. a cylinder, pyramid, or cube) from which more complex objects can be built.

Quad A four-point polygon.

Raycasting A simplified form of raytracing, where the effects of direct light on a model is traced by the rendering engine, but not the effects of light bouncing off or between surfaces.

Raytracing A rendering algorithm that simulates the physical and optical properties of light rays as they reflect off a 3D model, producing realistic shadows and reflections.

Real-time An operation where the computer calculates and displays the results as the user watches. Real-time rendering, for example, enables the user to move around a 3D scene or remodel objects on the screen without having to wait for the display to update.

Refraction The effect where rays of light are bent, typically when passing through one medium to another, such as air to water.

Rendering The process of creating a 2D image from 3D geometry to which lighting effects and surface textures have been applied.

Scale A 3D transformation that shrinks or enlarges an object about one or more axes.

Shading The process of filling in the polygons of a 3D model with respect to viewing angle and lighting conditions so that it resembles a solid object.

Skin In 3D applications, a surface stretched over a series of "ribs", such as an aircraft wing.

Specular map In 3D applications, a texture map—such as those created by noise filters—that is used instead of specular color to control highlights.

Stitching A technique in NURBS modeling whereby two or more surfaces are joined along their boundaries.

Surface In 3D applications, the matrix of control points and line end points underlying a mapped texture or color.

Sweep The process of creating a 3D object by moving a 2D profile along a path.

Texture The surface definition of an object.

Triangle The simplest type of polygon, made from three connected vertices.

UV coordinates In a 3D environment, a system of rectangular 2D coordinates used to apply a texture map to a 3D surface.

Vertex Another name for a point (polygons) or control point (NURBS).

View A window in a 3D program depicting the 3D scene from a given vantage.

Wireframe A skeletal view of a computer-generated 3D object before the surface rendering has been applied.

Z-Buffer A 3D renderer that solves the problem of rendering two pixels in the same place (one in front of the other) by calculating and storing the distance of each pixel from the camera (the "z-distance"), then rendering the nearest pixel last.

part 07. reference

INDEX

ACKNOWLEDGMENTS

PICTURE ACKNOWLEDGMENTS

Title Page   *Smoke*—Reinhard Claus

p2   *Look Up At The Sky*—Chen Qinfeng

p3   *Ajax*—Reinhard Claus

p12   *Jurassic Park*—Universal Pictures

p13   *Toy Story*—Disney/Pixar

p14   *Wolfenstein 3D*—iD Software

p15   *Return to Castle Wolfenstein*—iD
Software/Activision
Project Gotham Racing 2—Bizarre Creations

P16   *Daylight*—Chin Quinfeng

P32-33   All images—Chin Quinfeng

P36   Low Polygon game character—Dan Phillips

P38   *Final Fantasy: The Spirits Within*—Square Pictures/
Columbia Pictures
Major Damage—Chris Bailey

P39   *The Lord of the Rings: The Return of the King*—
New Line Studios

P56-57   *Plasma Cannon*—Brian Pace
Human 3D Models—Dan Phillips

P65   *Mousetrapped*—Ron Labbe, Studio 3D
Glassware with Limes—Invisible Ink, Sikroma SE

P87   Game character textures—Dan Phillips

GALLERY IMAGES

Thanks to Peder Aversten, Reinhard Claus, Jeremy Engleman,
Pavel Fedorchuk, Francois Gutherz, Kyoshi Harada, Derek Lea,
Bill Ledger, David Maas, Meats Meier, Dan Phillips, Carles Piles,
Chen Qinfeng, and Koji Yamagami.